David Lloyd:
How to Succeed in Business While Really Trying

by Richard Evans

David Lloyd:
How to Succeed in Business
While Really Trying

by Richard Evans

BLOOMSBURY

First published 1996 by Bloomsbury Publishing Plc,
2 Soho Square, London W1V 6HB

Copyright © by Richard Evans and David Lloyd 1996

The moral right of the author has been asserted

A copy of the CIP entry for this book is available from the British Library

ISBN 0 7475 2755 5

10 9 8 7 6 5 4 3 2 1

Typeset by Dorchester Typesetting Group Ltd
Printed by Clays Ltd, St Ives plc

Contents

Acknowledgements

Working in the slightly demented world of professional tennis makes constant movement a way of life but, even so, David Lloyd, over the past twelve months, has been moving faster and farther than ever. Suddenly places like Ghana and Australia have come within his orbit which, being located outside the range of his Ferraris, have forced him to take to the air more frequently than he would like. Keeping track of one's subject would have been impossible for a biographer had it not been for a cool head at mission control, in this case David's personal assistant Sally Andrews who always seemed to know which club or country Lloyd was likely to show up in next and was always ready to answer numerous queries. My heartfelt thanks.

To David and the entire Lloyd family, I am indebted for their patience and good humour. Even when the pressure was on and the situation with Whitbread was changing day by day. David made himself available, somehow, somewhere, on the end of his mobile which minimised the problems of re-writing against a tight deadline. Here I must also offer thanks to Kathy Rooney, Barnaby Hardent and the Bloomsbury staff for holding steady in the crunch. Even deep into the fifth set with the referee looking at his watch, there was never a hint of panic!

My thanks, too, for the co-operation I received from all the managers and staff at the various David Lloyd Leisure centres as well as the numerous figures in the financial world for their insight. And to Charles Haswell and John Barrett a special word of appreciation for their help.

And none of this would have met any kind of deadline had it not been for the hours spent by my wife, Lynn, transcribing tapes, checking indexes and correcting errors. It would never have happened without her.

R.E. July 1996

Introduction

Unlike its counterpart on Centre Court, BBC Radio's No. 1 Court commentary box at Wimbledon is an eyrie situated high above the members' enclosure. Although there is an air-conditioning system of sorts, we tend to keep the window open when we are off air and, unless we are careful, the sounds of any animated conversation can drift down to the players fifty feet below.

One afternoon in 1989, I found myself closing that window in a hurry. And back in our control centre, the BBC's sound engineers Julian Walthar and Brian Prior were probably tearing off their head sets to protect burning ears.

David Lloyd was on his mobile.

This was not always a signal to reach for the ear plugs but Lloyd, who had been a member of the BBC Radio commentary team for almost as long as he had been busy turning himself from a tennis player into a builder of tennis clubs, was not inclined to let an idle moment pass. If coverage switched from our court to Centre Court or elsewhere, he would seize the moment to call one of his clubs and check on some urgent item of business.

On this particular occasion, he was returning a call to a representative of Barnet Council. The newest David Lloyd Leisure Centre at that time was situated in the Barnet area at Finchley and the official wanted to talk to Lloyd about a complaint he had received from a woman who lived opposite the club. She said the lights had been left on after 11.30 in contravention of the lease and he was supporting her. I don't know how aggressive the council representative became in the woman's defence because I was only hearing one end of the conversation. But it was enough to trigger the bristly bulldog spirit in Lloyd — the same kind of spirit that had helped Britain win a Davis Cup doubles against Italy on that very No. 1 Court about ten years earlier.

Suddenly Lloyd's voice rose several decibels.

'Right, you want to fight? So we'll fight. But I want to warn you of one thing first. I NEVER LOSE!'

The windows rattled as I closed them. It was a miracle the whole precarious edifice didn't collapse and flatten the members in their All England Club ties below.

Attempting diversionary tactics, the council representative apparently tried to duck that salvo and move to what he felt was safer ground. Wasn't it true, he asked, that the lease forbade non-members to use the club for their own functions and that just such a non-member had done precisely that a short while before? Poor man. He hadn't understood that Lloyd's shotgun was double-barrelled.

'I'll have you know,' came the withering reply, 'that the PRIME MINISTER is a member of my club!'

She was, too. Oh, was she ever! Finchley was not only Margaret Thatcher's constituency but she recognised a full-blooded, pull-yourself-up-by-the-boot-straps, self-made capitalist entrepreneur when she saw one and she had supported David Lloyd all the way. If there was ever a living, breathing example of everything she thought an Englishman should be, the subject of our story must have come very closely to the perfect role model.

Switch from the corner shop in Grantham to a sports shop in Southend, and you can get some idea of the similarity in backgrounds. No silver spoons at birth — just an instinctive idea of where to dig for gold. Lady Thatcher found hers in the House of Commons. David Lloyd searched for his on a tennis court. But one look at his vastly more talented younger brother John told him that, no matter how hard he tried — and being ready to bust a gut barely describes the effort he put into it — he would have to look elsewhere.

And so he had a dream, not quite in the Martin Luther King class, perhaps, but a little more practical. He took a long, hard look at his sport in Britain and saw what was missing. Players were one thing; coaches were another and, for the time being at least, he was not in a position to manufacture either. But there was a third element — a glaring omission which was helping to keep Britain down among the also-rans in the world game — facilities, courts, clubs, somewhere, for heaven's sake, to play!

Apart from Queen's Club, which was badly in need of a face-lift, and the Vanderbilt which, despite its chic clientele, was stuck behind an underground station in Shepherd's Bush, there were so few passably comfortable places to play tennis in Britain it was laughable. But Lloyd never saw the joke. He felt it was shameful and exasperating and, after learning something about how tennis clubs were run in Canada, decided he was going to do something about it.

This is the story of how he succeeded, a story of one man with a burning ambition and a furious determination overcoming all the whingeing pessimists and dubious money men and finally finding people, like Charles Haswell and John Barrett, who shared his dream and believed that he was the person to achieve it.

The result has turned out to be one of the most remarkable entrepreneurial triumphs of the past twenty years. Richard Branson could, perhaps, claim to be the leader in coming up with individual ideas that turned to gold, but he was making his first couple of quid while still at Stowe, a public school that educates young gentlemen up to the age of eighteen.

Lloyd left school at fifteen. Like Sir Terence Conran and Anita Roddick, two other highly successful self-made business giants, Lloyd never attended business school. From the age of sixteen, his classroom was the tennis court and the big wide world that went on around it. Tennis pros are accused today of seeing little except the airport, hotel room and stadium. And in between there are courtesy cars and flunkies to ensure they never get lost and never have to pick up a sock. Tennis was not like that when Lloyd set out. To pay his way, he learned how to sell his father's dresses out of a trunk to Zambians and Kenyans. Education comes pretty quickly that way even if you never get a diploma.

Now David Lloyd has more than a diploma. He is chairman of a string of sixteen leisure centres — the total will have grown by the time the ink hits this page — which are now owned by Whitbread. In the same week that the group offered £180 million for eighteen

Marriott Hotels in the UK, Whitbread offered another £180 million for Lloyd's clubs. David said 'fine and see ya' or words to that effect. So Whitbread came back to the bargaining table and said that there was no future in buying these clubs without the man who created them. So they talked, and this semi-educated, semi-successful tennis player who had started with nothing but a dream came away with an extra £21 million. Suddenly his picture was spread larger over the business columns of the *Financial Times* and other serious broadsheets than it ever had been over the sports pages. The City loved him. No wonder. His clubs had made money from Day One and had thrived throughout the recession. People who were forgoing the annual holiday and screaming poverty clung on to memberships that cost them £325 a year. Now membership lists are full before a new club opens its doors. David Lloyd and his managers must be doing something right. What? How? Read on . . .

DAVID LLOYD
TEN DO'S AND DON'TS

Do's
1. You must have an unquenchable Dream.
2. You must invest some of your own money.
3. When assessing your financial projections, take your budget income and reduce it by 30 per cent.
4. Take your expenditure figure and add 20 per cent. If it still stacks up, go for it.
5. Make sure you never lose your way. People will try and put you down; make sure you are not put off.
6. You must learn very quickly who your friends really are.
7. When you know who you can trust, bring them into the business and give them responsibility.
8. You must have very good reporting systems (daily), both income and expenditure.
9. You must have strict financial controls. You should insist your signature is required on everything.
10. You don't have to be liked, but you must be respected to get your staff on your side.

Don'ts
1. Don't let the lawyers interfere with the business. They should only handle the legal side.
2. Don't relinquish more than 49 per cent at the beginning.
3. Don't let your heart rule your head. Everything must be judged on its own merit.
5. Don't keep staff who are unhappy or under-performing. Act quickly.
6. Don't trust anyone until they have earned that trust.
7. Don't ask staff to do a job that you can't do yourself.
8. Don't run the business from the office. Lead from the front.
9. Don't get sucked into all these new training methods. Your gut feel will be right more often than wrong.
10. Don't be frightened when trying new ideas.

Chapter 1

The Arena

The Arena is spacious but hardly flashy. It's not an arena, actually, at least not the part that is now occupied through five storeys by the executive offices of the David Lloyd Leisure Group. You could find it by mistake if you missed the turning for the M4 coming out of Heathrow — easily done by those picking up a rental car — because the Arena is situated off one of those arterial highways that snake around Hounslow, Feltham and Heston; boroughs caught in the slipstream of the world's busiest international airport.

You could miss the boss, too, once you are through the glass security doors of this unprepossessing office block. He's the short, stocky one in a Marks & Spencer jumper and open-necked shirt carrying the coffee mug out of the lift, looking mildly lost at that nine o'clockish hour before secretaries have got themselves organised.

Upstairs in the director's suite the man who created this empire, beginning with his first club just down the road at Heston, sits behind a large desk in a large room bereft of any trappings of opulence. Utility is the word that comes to mind and that will be music to the ears of the shareholders who now have a stake in one of the fastest-growing businesses in Britain — a stake in David Lloyd's dream.

Seventy people work here — architects, project managers, accountants, sales and marketing people — the tip of an iceberg that now stretches the length of Britain, from Chigwell to Cardiff to Glasgow, employing over a thousand people. These will not be ordinary people because they do not work for an ordinary man. If you know David Lloyd, almost the first thing you realise is that he will not tolerate around him people who are not loyal, dedicated and totally committed to the cause. Scores of them, especially in the early days, didn't make the grade. Some of these will tell you tales of Lloyd being a tough, terse boss who expected everyone to put in the kind of hours he did in the beginning — all hours, backbreaking hours.

'When Heston opened, I was the manager and I never left the place for a year,' he tells you. 'Maybe one day off in 365. There was so much to do, so much to learn. But I loved it.'

That is the bottom line, really. He loves it. And if his managers and senior staff don't truly love it too it will show and they won't last. Nor will his members. Although he is better now — better at keeping the fury and indignation under some sort of control — there will be many ex-members of Heston who will tell you that Lloyd was impossible in the early days.

Roger Becker, the former British Davis Cup player and coach, who remained a good friend throughout the turbulent early years, chuckles when he remembers how it was. 'David couldn't handle the criticism from some of the members if he felt it was unfair,' Becker recalls. 'Occasionally he'd just turn round and say "OK, if you don't like it here, then here's your money back and you can piss off!' He takes everything very personally. It's all emotion with David.'

Becker was almost right. A huge part of Lloyd's drive, energy and vision is borne along on a floodtide of emotion. So much so that many a cold-eyed CEO will wonder how on earth this little ball of fire managed to build such a stable empire without first engulfing himself and his dream in a mass of flames. The answer lies in Lloyd's total belief in what he was doing and the tennis player's ability to keep his eye on the ball. That and an instinctive feeling for figures. He may have left school at fifteen, but the correspondence course in business and book-keeping which he took while still a teenager came easily to him. And it immediately paid dividends when Lloyd began dealing with the money men.

John Barrett, who has filled so many roles in British tennis as well as being something of a father figure to Lloyd, remembers being flabbergasted by David's performances in board meetings. 'I used to sit there open-mouthed while David ran rings round all these highly trained accountants. He is an absolute genius with figures.'

Emotion-packed ambition, coupled with a brain that can handle numbers more inventively and just as accurately as a high-powered calculator, is a deadly combination and it proved too potent a force for all the nay-saying pessimists that he ran into while trying to conjure up the funds for his first venture near London Airport. For although Lloyd was setting out on a path that would make him a millionaire while really trying, the millions weren't the ultimate goal. It was his dream that drove him. The desire to be a success; the desire to prove that his ideas were valid and would work; the desire to prove wrong the people he did not respect. The ego. No champion, be it on a tennis court or in a board room, can operate successfully without an outsized ego; an ego big enough and tough enough to take a battering and survive. That's what Muhammad Ali and John McEnroe and Daley Thompson put up as a prize. I am the best. I will win. These are incredibly brave statements from anyone competing in the public arena or in front of a room full of business associates. Because you have to face those same people if you lose or fail. And, at some time or other, everyone fails. And then, for the true competitor, there is more than egg on the face. There is a dagger through the heart. There is pain, real pain. People cry because when you have stripped your ego bare and announced to the world that you are going to succeed, failure hurts. Perhaps Lloyd is a little bit different because his emotional makeup is such that he cries when he succeeds. When he stepped forward to make his speech at the opening of his first club at Heston, he didn't get through two sentences before the tears started to flow. Soon he was sobbing and had to stop. I will never forget that. It was then I knew just what the whole thing meant to David Lloyd. He had put everything on the line — his reputation, his mortgage, his family's future, and he had won. He is a very, very emotional man.

Lloyd has a thousand stories to tell about how he built his empire and he tells them fast, in that chirpy Essex accent, punctuated at intervals by the aggressive body language of the street fighter but softened by the larrikin's lopsided grin. The following tale encapsulates a lot of what David Lloyd is all about, revealing much of what he believes and what he expects and just how much, or how little, he will accept. It also shows how he had to re-evaluate relationships in the business world and learn to become a bit more like a politician than a do-or-die competitor in a sporting arena. He discovered that supposed enemies were often only professional antagonists who would share a drink in the bar later. Lew Hoad and Rod Laver and John Newcombe could have taught him that because it was the great Australian creed, but somehow David had always been too much of a firebrand to take note of that concept during his playing days and now, initially to his cost, he was to discover that it was true in all walks of life, all the way up to the peak in politics.

We were talking about Lady Thatcher's involvement with the Finchley Club and how she had been there to open it before taking out her membership and Lloyd let his mind run with the story:

'Yes, she was great. She still comes down with Denis occasionally but we still have our battles with a representative of Barnet Council. The lease stated "It's a private members club" so again you have to be a little careful. At the end of the day, any rule can be broken or twisted — which we don't like to do. And I said to the guy later on, "if you want us to break that rule legally, all you do is you don't have a guest form, you have a daily membership form. You can't stop me from doing that. But I don't want to do that." So, we win a few battles and lose a few battles. We still have shouting matches with one man. The thing that gets you is when you go around to meet him, he's a nice guy. He's as nice as can be, really.

It struck when John and I went to one of those charity boxing matches at the Hilton. It was just when we were starting to get well-known and we sat next to Harold Wilson who told us all sorts of stories about Parliamentary life. He was in power at the time and had these raging arguments in the House of Commons with Ted Heath who was Leader of the Opposition. And it seemed that they hated each other. But Wilson said that he quite liked Heath really, that they used to have drinks together afterwards. I remember being amazed at that. But, later, I got to learn that solicitors do the same.

We took two coaches to court or they took us to court. I'll never forget it — it was very sad. At Heston, we used to have a day of cleaning every year and we'd close the club to members and all the paid staff came in — workers, pros, management — we all came in. It was like a spring cleaning. We did all the things you can't do during a normal day's cleaning. We had things mended and had a lovely lunch. John Barrett came in his track suit and he was scrubbing. Everyone got together and was sweeping up. And it was good. But two pros said, "We're not coming in" and I said, "Fine. I can't force you to come in. But, by the way, don't come back Monday because you don't have any courts. That's the deal." So they said, "Fine" and they didn't come back. But then about four or five weeks later we got a letter saying that Mr Hugh Latham and Mr Tom Morgan have been unfairly dismissed. But I thought, wait a minute, they can't be unfairly dismissed because they were not employed here in the first place. I haven't filled in tax forms for them. They're just freelance teaching pros who hire courts from me. So we went to court — to an industrial tribunal and the solicitor said, "We can't lose for this, that and the other reason. We don't fill in their tax form. They are self-employed. No problem." So, I'm sitting there in this sort of briefing room before the thing starts. I'd never actually been to an industrial tribunal before — I'd only read about them. And my barrister got out of the car with another guy — so I said "Who was that guy?" and he said, "That's the other barrister" and I said "What were you doing?" so then he said, "I think we should settle" so I said, "What do you mean settle? You've been telling me for the last four months that I can't lose! Now you get out of the car with the other guy and say settle." So I said, "No, we're going in." And we went in and lost. We were going to lose because the guy asked one thing — "Do they work at the club more than sixteen hours a week?" and I said, "Yes" and he said, "Well, that's employment." So, I knew we had no chance and settled. I had to pay each of them £15,000 and I said to my guy, "Look, I'm not paying you one cent — not a penny. And if you want a penny, I'll sue you. Because if you, as a solicitor, cannot find out one basic rule about sixteen hours and explain it to me, then you are not doing your job. You are *an employment barrister." And he knew it, that's why he didn't want me to go in there — he wanted to get his piece and settle. And it broke my heart. Not about the money. The principle.*

The sad thing from the pros' point of view — the reason I backed down was because if that case had gone against us, every coach in this country would have been nailed because most coaches are self-employed. To these guys who had been self-employed, they just wouldn't be earning — because of taxes. But, if they're employed, the club couldn't afford to have them employed for the same amount of money — and so suddenly, it could have put all the coaches in this country out of work. So that's why I said, "Fine. Here's the fifteen grand." It was my judgement. I mean, they are self-employed. They are there only sixteen hours — think about it; they go off and play a tournament whenever they want to, and for our purpose it is absolutely, 100 per cent normal self-employment. Then there are other people who are just thieves. The hardest part of my business is when the people who steal my money are my friends. I couldn't take it — even if it were only a penny. But that's another story . . .'

Chapter 2

Dennis and Doris + John

'I had to go and see the headmaster to tell him David was leaving school at fifteen. He thought I was stark raving mad, of course. He didn't know what tennis was.'

Dennis Lloyd, settling comfortably into a chair on the porch of John's house at the Sunrise Country Club at Rancho Mirage, California, permits himself a little chuckle, as well he might. This is a man who took a radical, controversial decision about his son's education and now winters here with his wife, Doris. The golf course stretches away behind him as we talk; the March temperature nudges 26.5°C (80°F) and the tips of the San Jacinto mountains, still white with snow, glisten in the afternoon sun. They call this corner of California the Desert Kingdom although the only royalty around here appears to be Bob Hope, Frank Sinatra, Gerald Ford and Dinah Shore, all of whom have long, connecting roads named after them.

Typically directions to one of the numerous sprawling country clubs that have sprung up on desert scrub over the past twenty years follow the lines of 'Take Bob Hope to Frank Sinatra and turn left on Gerald Ford' — only in America. In this instance, although there is an entrance to Sunrise on Bob Hope, it is best to use the one on Country Club Drive where an armed guard will check your identity at the gate, raise the barrier and allow you to enter this hidden world of one-storey homes, clustered around the golf course, shielded by flora and towering palms. In the summer months the temperatures soar to absurd heights that touch 60°C (140°F), but from October to April it is a virtual paradise for those wishing to escape the noise and pollution of a big city or the winter winds that whip off the North Sea along the Essex coast.

Even after a few years of travel, John Lloyd was still English to the core in the mid-Seventies when he first set eyes on this area that is still loosely referred to as Palm Springs. He was playing in the American Airlines Tennis Games — the forerunner of Charlie Pasarell's Newsweek Cup at Indian Wells — which had been transferred from Tucson, Arizona to the newly developed Mission Hills Country Club at Rancho Mirage, another desert city just down Highway 111 from Palm Springs. Anything out of reach of British newspapers and the football scores, especially details of all Wolverhampton Wanderers' matches, was still anathema to young John, but the story goes that a Hollywood actress with a considerable appetite for life might have had something to do with altering his view of the place. Their meeting was brief but you could say it was an eye-opener and, by the time he married Chris Evert, the idea of buying a house in the desert was something that appealed to him — especially as he had discovered a local newsagent who could supply the *Daily Mail* only one day late.

It was not long after he bought the place that John invited his parents to spend long stretches of the winter there to escape the English chill. A visitor to the Lloyd home at Sunrise in the early spring of 1996 would have found that time had moved on. John, the celebrity years of marriage to Chrissie long behind him, now has two young children by his second American wife, Deborah. His father, less active than he used to be, had just taken his first tentative steps back onto the tennis court after a bout with cancer. John had been hitting balls at him in a gentle arc just so that Dennis could get the feel of the ball on the racket strings again. There had been remedial exercises in the pool too, but there was no aura of crisis or tragedy hanging over this household. The children ran about; Doris was in and out of the kitchen; John, now coach to Britain's Davis Cup team under the captaincy of his brother, discussed the possibility of Tim Henman reaching the top twenty on the ATP computer and the cheeky grin that David had inherited from his father was still very much in evidence on Dennis's face.

One needed to go back in time to learn where it all started; this passion for a game that led Dennis and Doris Lloyd to produce three boys all of whom would end up playing at Wimbledon. Had not an equally remarkable family on the other side of the world been harbouring similar ambitions, the Lloyds would have been unique in producing three sons capable of playing to Wimbledon standard. But Robert and Maggie Amritraj raised Anand, Vijay and Ashok at approximately the same time in Madras, and long before they were able to set off for their early morning runs down Sterling Road, Maggie had pre-determined their destiny. 'I was determined they would all be champions of India and then play at Wimbledon,' she said. And, of course, they did.

Dennis was not quite so specific in his goals, possibly because there were so many other options open to children growing up in the densely populated area of Essex around Southend, Westcliffe and Leigh-on-Sea. Nevertheless tennis had become the family game long before the boys followed their older sister Anne out of the cot. It had, in fact, become Dennis's game even before he met Doris at a cricket match in Durham where he was posted during the Second World War.

Showing all the signs of independence and initiative that would later manifest themselves in David, young Dennis Lloyd, a fifteen-year-old grammar schoolboy with a father who ran his own cricket team, went off cycling around the lanes between Romford and his home one fine summer's Sunday afternoon and came across Gidea Park Tennis Club.

'I knew nothing about tennis at that stage,' Dennis recalls. 'I was a fair cricketer and footballer, played for Essex schoolboys and that sort of thing, but tennis was a completely foreign game to me until I passed this club and stopped to take a look. I hung over the fence for a bit and thought, hmm, this looks like quite a good game. So I got a few of my school friends together and we decided to go and join the club. We ended up forming a sort of junior section, really, and just learned the rules by watching other people. We never worried about tactics or anything. We just ran after the ball and tried to get it back. It was on clay courts so it wasn't too fast and we just ran and ran all day. That was about 1936 or so, and by the time the war came along, I was in the first team and starting to be not a bad player.'

Interestingly, the members of Gidea Park were open-minded

enough to let the children in and give them court time, something that is not always the case in some of Britain's tennis clubs even today. 'No, I don't remember there being any problem about being accepted,' says Dennis. 'Maybe some didn't exactly welcome us with open arms but there was no real opposition, although I remember a few grumblings a couple of years later on when some of us started pushing people out of the club teams!'

While sport fired Dennis's competitive spirit, the young lad could find little to enthuse over in the classroom and it was with resignation as much as anger that his headmaster told him one day, 'You know, Lloyd, you do so little work here, you'll end up digging trenches.'

Dennis still chuckles at the memory. 'He was right, too, but not quite in the way he imagined. Working on the roads, being a navvy as it was called in those days, was considered the lowest form of life and I never quite stooped to that, but as soon as you join the Army you quickly find out they have all sorts of jobs for you.'

Like thousands of teenagers all over Britain, Dennis Lloyd found himself being called up on September 1st 1939 and told to report to South Street, Romford, headquarters of the 134th Field Regiment Territorials. There, in a perfect preview of *Dad's Army*, David's Dad was given an extra sixpence a week allowance because he had a raincoat — in lieu of the uniforms which hadn't quite arrived — handed a shovel and told to start digging out air raid shelters.

'I thought, hang on a minute, that headmaster was dead right! So our lot — 340 Artillery Battery, I think we were — set about digging these air raid shelters without proper boots and the shovels broke and the whole thing was a shambles, a complete shambles. It didn't get much better either. Not for a long time. Much later in the war we were moved to another barracks — nothing more than a collection of depressing huts, really — near Blenheim. It was sort of on the edge of a forest and it was very damp. Mud and pools of water everywhere, pretty awful sort of place. But we couldn't get away from the digging. My section was given three bent shovels and told to dig out a path. Our uniforms still weren't up to much but I think I had managed to acquire a pair of gumboots to keep out some of the water by this stage. We were still appallingly equipped. No wonder Hitler was feeling pretty cocky. At any rate we took about a week to dig this path that couldn't have been more than fifty yards long.

'Then one night we were woken by an almighty roar and we peeked out and saw all these headlights and huge armoured vehicles and jeeps and bulldozers bursting in all over the place and we realised the Americans had arrived. Blimey, you never saw anything like it. At least we hadn't. Big black blokes with large cigars sitting up in the cabins of these huge vehicles. We'd never seen any black people except in the pictures. It was amazing. And then they set to and proceeded to build an entire airstrip in the time it had taken us to dig fifty yards of gravel!'

It was the sort of experience that prepared Dennis in some small way for his present surroundings — a fragrant, watered desert oasis with the manicured ninth green of a dream-like golf course a ditch's dig away from his front porch. It took him a decade or two to make the transition from Pte Lloyd digging trenches in the damp English countryside to luxuriating in the amenities of the Sunrise Country Club, but by then his belief in the American ability to create anything out of nothing was secure. Still quintessentially English, Dennis Lloyd's irrepressible sense of humour has entertained his American cronies in the desert with stories such as these over many a dinner in recent years when, until her recent death, his companions included Ginger Rogers.

'Lovely lady,' he remembers. 'Lived just across the golf course over there and used to enjoy a night out with our little group.'

Fred Astaire's famous dancing partner would have enjoyed being waltzed through Dennis's fertile memory, tracking the absurdities of British life in the war. No one born too late to have lived through those times can quite grasp the upheaval it wrought on an essentially staid and stay-at-home society, deeply entrenched in its class distinctions and social mores. Fate and the lives caught up in it swirled with the unpredictability of a gale in the English Channel and one such twist sent the Essex boy north to Newcastle and a meeting with the girl who would become his life-long companion.

'We were sent up to Newcastle to be ready for embarkation for

France until word came through that, far from trying to get any more in, they were trying to get everyone out. It was 1940. Dunkirk. So they told us to stay where we were which was actually Durham by that time. Then they came and took away all our guns, all our rifles, just about everything. They left us one gun as a sort of token gesture for an artillery unit. They needed them for the defence of London, I suppose. Anyway, there we were and because the world was coming to an end and Hitler had just taken the whole of Europe, we decided to have a cricket match. It seemed like an appropriate sort of thing to do. So we played a local miners' team at Burn Moor, and during the knock-up when we were just out on the field practising a bit of batting and bowling, this lovely young girl of about seventeen comes along and hands one of their chaps a sandwich and a piece of cake. I noticed her as she walked out and thought, mmm, she's not bad, and then I didn't think any more of it. But we met up again later and that was it. We got married, Anne, our first child, was born in Newcastle while the war was still on and then I took them south. We've been together over fifty-two years now. Amazing, isn't it?'

Almost as amazing was the fact that Dennis had survived the war at all, or that anyone in his unit did for that matter. Having had their Lee Enfields taken away, the 134th were issued with something called a Ross rifle which had been made in Canada.

'And not recently, either,' he continued. 'First World War jobs. So stiff you couldn't open the bloody bolt. By the time you could have got it working, you would have been dead! The next thing they gave us were French 75's, artillery guns with which we were supposed to blow up one of our own fighter airstrips. There was a panic on about the Germans parachuting in and then taking over our airfields — if they had landed God knows what we would have done — so the idea was that we would blow the place up as soon as our aircraft had taken off. The problem was — well, there were several problems, really. First of all half of the shells went round the corner when you fired them, which was no wonder because when we looked down the barrel we saw that these things had been made in 1914 and last calibrated in 1918.

'Anyway, we were supposed to practise this great assault on the airstrip but how could we? There were houses all around us and we were supposed to be using live shells! The whole thing was ridiculous, a complete farce.'

It was obviously Dennis's sense of humour that got him through it — the British sense of humour that was a not inconsiderable weapon in a war against the Nazi mentality. They never did find out what it was that kept us laughing. But there was one aspect of the war that angered Dennis for, just like David, the elder Lloyd has a deep-seated dislike of being deceived.

'None of us really wanted to be running around playing soldiers but we got on with it. What really did make me mad was the way the Government kept so much from us. They KNEW Germany was re-arming. They KNEW what Hitler was up to. God alone knows Churchill tried to tell them. He tried to tell us as well but the Government branded him a warmonger. I suppose a lot of us, still remembering the First War, just didn't want to believe it. But it was the Government's duty to warn us what was going on and they didn't because they were afraid of public reaction. That's not leadership. That's cowardice. It's one thing if you don't know. If you're deluded you're deluded, but to conceal things of that importance is wicked.'

The fire has not died in Dennis Lloyd. Not the advancing years, nor the attack of cancer, nor even the soft spring breezes that waft through the Coachella Valley can quell the alertness and vitality of the man and, in many ways, to know the father is to know the son. Or at least the eldest son. No one in the family makes any bones about the fact that John and Tony are very different personalities. But Dennis and David are two peas from the same family pod — in build, outlook, humour, personality. They speak the same way and take offence at the same things. Both have a will of iron.

David was born on January 3rd 1948 at Woodfield Road, Leigh-on-Sea, much to the delight of Dennis's friend Damon Millett, a tennis historian who pointed out that the young lad would share a birthday with the great Willie Renshaw who had turned Wimbledon into his own private hunting ground in the 1880s by winning the Championship singles title seven times in nine years. Any idea that this was just a fanciful notion on Millett's part was dismissed with an air of supreme confidence. 'Your wife's maiden name is Renshaw!' he told Dennis. 'The coincidence is just too great. David will definitely be a tennis player.' Dennis did not need much persuading and from then on David's course in life was set. 'You wouldn't have had much option in our household,' he laughs. 'There was no way of avoiding tennis. At dinner my parents would talk about little else.'

Monday to Friday, however, Dennis had plenty else to think about because, by the time David was born, he was well established in his father's export business in the City. At the beginning they exported just about any financially plausible merchandise to various parts of the world; raw materials, bicycles, dresses and garments of various kinds. But eventually the company with its headquarters near the Guildhall started to specialise in textiles and Africa became its prime market. On the death of David's grandfather, Herbert Henry Lloyd, Dennis took over the running of the company and throughout the Fifties it prospered. But Harold Macmillan's 'Winds of Change' speech in Africa changed more than the political landscape. Decolonisation meant that nations which had been painted pink on those maps schoolchildren used to work from in class suddenly realised they were no longer obligated to import just from the 'mother' country and, sooner than many people had expected, the winds of change were blowing through the trading houses along London Wall.

But that didn't happen until the mid-Sixties and by then the Lloyd family at Leigh-on-Sea was growing. John and Tony followed David and it was soon evident that Mr and Mrs Lloyd would have no trouble getting their children to share their passion for sport. The boys played everything at school but tennis had become Dennis's first love and he soon had his sons hitting at the local club. Long before John's graceful, God-given talents began to emerge, David flung himself into his sport with the zest of a little pit bull terrier. And not just his sport. Life for young David was something to be seized by the throat.

'The amount of energy he had was, frankly, frightening at times,' admits his father, 'the energy and the bloody-minded determination to have his own way. Occasionally he needed a good whack. I had to discipline him far more than the other boys. I felt I really had to stand up to him otherwise it could have all gone wrong. If you don't learn how to control and channel that kind of energy and will-power at an early age, it's not long before you start having problems.'

Young David was fortunate in that he had two things going for him — a love of a highly disciplined sport and a father who encouraged him to take it seriously. Doris played a major role as well. With her husband coming back late in the evening from the City, fighting the rush hour at Liverpool Street Station and the unpredictability of British Rail on the run down to the Essex coast, Doris had time to fill with the children after school and much of that time was spent on a tennis court.

'For a number of years she played with them more than I did,' says Dennis. 'She was a good player herself and helped them a lot. I used to take over at weekends and, as they grew, I enjoyed playing with each of them in tournaments and such like. I played more serious tennis with David than the others mainly because I was younger when he was in his early teens and we used to have some good battles. He soon became the No. 1 junior in our area and when he was twelve or thirteen I used to partner him against the best club players around. I was about county standard, as good or better than most of the opposition, so obviously they played on David. No one likes getting beat by a thirteen-year-old so they gave him as hard a time as they could. That's fine. I think it was good training for him. They're not going to give you anything and you don't get it and you learn the hard way. I think I helped all the boys by playing with them competitively because they all became good doubles players.'

You can detect the pride in his voice as he relates this story and the pride is not misplaced. Dennis combined the roles of father and coach — up to a point. And it is that point which so many tennis fathers miss or just plain ignore. Although, inevitably, there have been exceptions which prove the rule — Sergi Bruguera's father, Luis, being one of the most obvious* — too many parents of bud-

*Bruguera, who won the French Open in 1993 & 1994 and has been ranked as high as No. 3 in the world, is still coached by his father.

ding juniors hang on too long and cosset their sons and daughters to an extent that they not only impede their progress and stifle the very talent they are trying to nurture but can also, in the most extreme cases, create several emotional problems.

This is a serious subject, possibly the single most important issue facing professional tennis today. The horror stories of children being abused by parents who use their offspring as vehicles for the fulfilment of their own fantasies are all too common. In America there have been suicides at tennis camps, and no one with even peripheral knowledge of the game needs to be told of the beatings Mary Pierce took from her father as a teenager — Jim Pierce is now banned from attending tournaments — or of Jennifer Capriati's cry for help that took her off into the world of drugs and rock 'n' roll so soon after she had won Olympic Gold in Barcelona.

Male players have come under parental sway and, although there is no question of any abuse, the tennis world is waiting to see when Nick Philippoussis decides that the time has come for him to step back and for his hugely talented son, Mark, to put himself in the hands of any number of highly qualified Australian coaches who are ready to help the young giant fulfil his considerable potential, building upon the firm foundations laid by his father.

All parents who are finding it difficult to let go should spend a little time talking to Dennis Lloyd. Here was a man who was a player of reasonable ability — certainly as good as some of the so-called ex-players I used to see masquerading as coaches on the pro tour in the Seventies — who had three talented sons, all of whom wanted to make tennis a career. The temptation for their father to try and take them all the way into the pro ranks may not have been as great as it would have been today, with the huge sums of money on offer, but it was still a temptation. But Dennis never really gave it a thought. Right from the start his only concern was to find someone with more ability and more contacts than he had who could help his sons get a foot on the tennis ladder. To begin with he enlisted the services of a coach nearby in Essex called Lionel Bradford who, being a bit ahead of his time, stressed the nutritional side of an athlete's training and tried to keep David on a proper diet. But Dennis always knew that he would have to reach higher.

'By the time David started playing Junior Wimbledon, I knew I had to find someone to take him to the next level. In those days it was essential to have the right contacts, someone who could get a kid into the official circle with proper training and access to practice courts at Queen's Club and that sort of thing. Before David had left school I used to go to the headmaster to get him off on Wednesday afternoons to travel all the way across London for a coaching session at Queen's. By the time he got there all the best boys had gone and he was left to push balls back and forth with the girls. That was no good. So the day David was to play Gerald Battrick in the final of Junior Wimbledon, I took the plunge and approached John Barrett who was already British Davis Cup captain and someone who was obviously interested in developing British juniors.

'So I went up to him as we were standing down there at the bottom of the All England Club where the clay courts used to be — because the tournament was always played on clay — and said, "Excuse me, Mr Barrett, you don't know me from Adam but I'm David Lloyd's Dad. He'll probably lose 3 and 2 today because Gerald's a better clay court player but he's dead keen and I can only take him so far. Could you do me the favour of taking a look at him and, if you think he has any potential, perhaps you could take him on." Well, I don't know if John remembers any of this but he said he would and then the Barrett Boys were formed shortly afterwards and David was on his way.'

John Barrett remembers it well. 'I was impressed right away by the fact that Dennis was aware of his own time limitations, because he had a business to run, as well as his lack of coaching experience at the highest level,' says Barrett. 'If only all tennis parents would have as much foresight and self-discipline.'

Barrett had been a fringe Davis Cup player himself after coming down from Cambridge in an era when Britain actually had some tennis players worthy of the name — Mike Davies, Bobby Wilson, Billy Knight and Roger Becker being the best before Mike Sangster came along. But it was off court that JB, as he is known to his friends, had the biggest influence on British tennis — an influence that many people feel should have continued longer than it did.

Barrett enjoyed the schoolmasterish role he adopted towards a group of Britain's best young talent and formed what became known as the Barrett Boys. It was funded partly by the Lawn Tennis Association and partly by the parents themselves, Dennis chipping in for some of the expenses. The whole idea got started soon after the tragically early death of George Worthington, the Australian who died of cancer in 1963 after a successful and highly popular period as coach to the All England Club and Britain's Davis Cup squads. 'George's death created a void which no one seemed capable of filling so I decided something needed to be done,' says Barrett. For the record, the group comprised Battrick who, with Graham Stilwell, was probably the most talented of the nine who made up the original batch, John Clifton, Paul Hutchins, Keith Wooldridge, Peter Curtis, Clay Iles, Stanley Matthews, son of the great footballer, and David Lloyd.

After Dennis Lloyd's plea for assistance at Wimbledon, Barrett had no hesitation in including David in the group. 'At one stage I thought he would turn out to be the best of the lot,' admits Barrett. 'He had this tremendous spirit and aggression. I was always impressed by the energy coming from the lad. He was wild in a lot of ways; wild hair, wild attitude to a lot of things, but on court he reminded me of a shorter Frank Sedgman in that he had that pigeon-toed walk and dynamic sort of game. But there was always a backhand weakness that we could never really cure and, of course, good players soon discovered that and exploited it.'

Dennis Lloyd had spotted that weakness early and, as a nine-year-old, David was being told to hit backhands and stop running round to club his forehand. 'But, instinctively, he didn't want to do it,' recalls Dennis. 'No matter what I said, he would use his speed to get around onto his forehand. He really had a tough time with it because he had this enormous desire to show me how well he could hit the ball and, at that stage, he could only do that on the forehand. I kept telling him, "We're not here to work on what you're good at but what you're bad at." But it was tough getting him to listen.'

The first time David was taken over to the Queen's Club for a session with an LTA coach, he was told he was hitting his forehand much too square on. 'The man was obsessed with trying to change my forehand which was easily my best shot and he totally ignored my backhand,' David recalls. 'That's been the trouble with so much of the coaching in Britain — too much done by what is supposed to be the book and not enough taught from practical experience. But, in any case, Dad's right. I should have paid greater attention to what he was trying to get me to do.'

Nevertheless, once he was put in Barrett's care, David's career was off and running — literally. The Barrett Boys were housed at the Wimbledon YMCA and JB used to call soon after 7.00 a.m. and drive them up the hill to Wimbledon Common for their early morning run. 'He used to make us run in boots to build up our leg muscles,' David recalls. 'It was tough but it was great training.'

From 9.30, the boys were on court all morning, often under the added supervision of Tony Mottram, father of Buster, who had been No. 1 in Britain himself just a few years before and who was brought in to talk technique. Three days a week there was circuit training and, in their spare time, everyone followed correspondence courses — Clay Iles in journalism, Wooldridge taking his A levels, Lloyd with his bookkeeping studies. Barrett never ignored the need to keep their minds on matters other than tennis. But, inevitably, with a group of spirited, individualistic youngsters living together, there were a few escapades that got back to the hierarchy at the LTA who were funding the scheme and Barrett had to go and doff his cap.

Come springtime, Barrett would pile his Boys into three station-wagons provided by Ford and drive down to the South of France and the kind of paradise that awaited tournament players in those days; five or six weeks in the Riviera sunshine at such places as Beaulieu, Menton, Monte Carlo, Nice and Cannes. The days of Hemingway and Scott Fitzgerald were long gone but something of that aura lingered amongst the palms and bougainvillaea. Personalities such as Ted Tinling, with his innate sense of the traditions of the game, and his design partner Henry Turner were omnipresent figures at the tournaments, fussing over details of dress and protocol and enlivening the evening's gatherings with their wit and laughter. The game was still played in white flannels and, with the austerity of the war years receding, a little glamour was returning to the great hotels along the coast. The tennis on the slow red clay was demanding as there was always a gaggle of French, Spanish and South Americans who could run all day and test one's technique to its limits. 'And a Hungarian,' commented Wimbledon referee Alan Mills who was playing on the circuit in those days. 'Istvan Gulyas was incredible. He got to the French final around that time and set the standard for clay court expertise during those tournaments on the Riviera.'

Patrick Proisy, now one of Mark McCormack's top agents with IMG in Paris, and Jean-Claude Barclay, he of the spectacles and the weird grip, were two of the Frenchmen, a third was their clay court master François Jauffret. But it is the fellow you can still see waddling around the ATP Tour with his pot-belly encased in a rumpled track suit that most of the Barrett Boys will remember as their most frustrating opponent. Pato Alvarez was known as Willy in those days but he hasn't changed that much. The Colombian with the lop-sided grin has simply switched from being a wheeling-dealing player, who entrepreneurially sold pieces of equipment out of the back of his car, to a wheeling-dealing coach who has masterminded the careers of Emilio Sanchez and his long-time doubles partner Sergio Casal. The rumpled look is deceptive as are so many other things about Alvarez. Even by the standards of today's superstars, the man is rich. He owns apartments in Spain and Colombia and once showed off his bank balance to a friend, revealing a healthy current account balance of over a million dollars.

'We all knew Willy was making money but we were more concerned about working out a way of beating him,' Barrett recalls. 'He was the ultimate clay court wizard, always having another trick up his sleeve and steady as a rock. I remember one match David had with him on the courts of the Carlton Hotel in Cannes. It went on forever with one rally I shall never forget lasting well over a hundred strokes because David was absolutely determined not to give in. But he couldn't beat him. I don't think any of our boys ever did.'

Afterwards, Alvarez would be his usual grinning self. 'I beat him easy,' he would chuckle. 'I lob. I pass. Easy.' Nothing against David Lloyd was ever quite as easy as that, but somehow Alvarez always had something on you, a feeling that is still difficult to shake, even to this day, when you bump into him in Monte Carlo or Barcelona. Open up the boot of his car and, one is convinced, boxes of shoes and packets of gut would come tumbling out. All in all, coming up against characters like Alvarez was an education for the Barrett Boys and they returned to England every year wiser and a little less intimidated by the realities of the continental game.

There were people at Baron's Court, however, who seemed jealous. Not merely of young lads who should have been at school living the high life on the Côte d'Azur but at the amount of control John Barrett had been given to conduct their careers. No doubt several members of the LTA Management Committee were nervous about it but one man, in particular, was never going to tolerate it for long.

Basil Reay seemed to be bureaucratically minded and had discovered that the disorganised world of lawn tennis was fertile ground for his activities. He began with British tennis but that was too easy; too malleable. Reay, small in stature with bushy eyebrows and a cynical laugh, soon was appointed General Secretary of the International Lawn Tennis Federation, as it was known in those days, while keeping his other job as secretary of the LTA. Suddenly he was involved with every aspect of the game world-wide. There was no ATP; no WTA; no professional organisation to oversee the sport. Just a far-flung bunch of National Association presidents who had other careers to worry about and knew far less about the workings of the game than Reay did. He was the only fully paid, full-time employee in amateur tennis and for a couple of decades nothing happened in the world game without Reay's stamp of approval.

Barrett was on a hiding to nothing with Reay and it was amazing the Barrett Boys were allowed to exist for as long as they did. 'In fact the whole thing would probably not have got off the ground had I not cooked up the scheme while Basil was away for several weeks in Australia,' Barrett admits. 'He might have shot it down in flames if the LTA committee had not agreed to it by the time he got back. It seemed that he wanted nothing that he could not control and he used to admit that he didn't really like tennis that much anyway. It seemed to me a disaster for the game that he had so much influence.' Eventually, JB was summoned to face the committee at Baron's Court one day to be told by Reay something along the lines of 'Been getting some bad reports about the behaviour of one or two of your chaps. Can't have that. Won't do at all. Have to disband the group, I'm afraid.'

So, with a swift executive order, Reay, backed by the LTA committee, dealt what was in my view another damaging blow to British tennis. Many experts felt that the Barrett Boys had been the best initiative seen in the game in this country since the war, but Reay seemed to feel otherwise. The reports, predictably enough, concerned Lloyd and Battrick who were inclined to let their frustration show by chucking the odd racket and generally behaving in a way that was considered intolerable by the LTA elders. Nothing awful, certainly nothing approaching the near anarchy of the Jimmy Connors-John McEnroe years, but just a bit too boisterous for the authorities. It could have been dealt with sensibly. But I feel that Reay was just looking for an excuse to close down the scheme.

'One needed to watch David because he was a driven sort of boy; highly strung, intense and he felt the pressure of expectation tremendously,' says Barrett of a youngster who was later to become a life-long friend. 'I think that's why he enjoyed doubles so much because the intensity of pressure isn't the same. But I enjoyed helping him and John, too, of course, a little later. I got to know the family really well. Dennis and I won the Slazenger veteran doubles at the Palace Hotel in Torquay in the days of the great tournaments down there. The next year we won it again at Eastbourne which was the last year the event was held, so we retired undefeated!'

Looking back on those days, Barrett, who was trying to be a track suit manager along the lines of the great Australian coach Harry Hopman and whose methods he had studied carefully, feels he made one basic mistake.

'I entered us all in tournaments and played against the Boys if the draw turned out that way,' he recalls. 'I think that was a mistake. I didn't realise at the time just how much unfair pressure I was putting on them. It was particularly difficult when I played David at Stalybridge indoors on TennisQuick and beat him. He overreacted wildly and cut all the strings out of his rackets.'

But, as is always the case with this emotional man, David quickly got over it and was soon proving to Barrett how much he appreciated his guidance. There was a Goods Manufacturers Sports Show at Olympia and on one of the stands they were offering prizes for the person who could keep a rally going longest. David was selected by JB to represent the Barrett Boys and, after winning the daily T-shirt, he went for the week's big prize, an expensive Breitling watch. Sure enough, after a phenomenal rally that seemed to go on forever, Lloyd won the watch and promptly gave it to Barrett.

'It was typical of his generosity,' says JB. 'He had a great sense of team spirit and didn't want to grab something just for himself. He had no money of his own at the time and that watch was worth a bit.'

John

Everyone says what an easy time John and Tony had in the Lloyd household compared to David. The rumbustious elder brother was always being disciplined and occasionally whacked — especially, on one occasion, when his big sister, Anne, reported him to his father for smoking. David hasn't forgotten that one. In contrast, Dennis was a lot easier on the two younger boys, not only because he was getting more used to the parental role and calming down a bit himself, but because John and Tony were such different personalities. The contrasts were stark and easily identifiable.

'If there was a conker up a tree, David would go up to the highest branch to get it,' John remembers. 'And while I'd be thinking, No, I don't like the look of that, he'd fall off and break his arm. He broke his arm two or three times. Neither Tony nor I ever had an injury as serious as that. We just tended to be a lot safer. We'd be on our bikes and he'd be haring down the hill not caring if a car was coming. I got a lot more scared than he did. David never got scared.'

There were differences with everyday things that gave an inkling of how the brothers would seek different paths to success in life, too — like pocket money. 'Somehow David always seemed to be able to make money grow. He had this ability to buy a bar of chocolate for, say, ten pence and sell it at a profit. He was doing that from a very young age. It wasn't like he was tight with his money, but he just seemed to have this knack of being able to triple and quadruple it. Amazing. I never understood that. I just spent mine. Still do.'

However, it was precisely because he was so different that John, a cherubic-looking little blond chap in his nicely pressed school uniform, had such a tough time when he turned up for his first day at Southend High School. Being the unpleasant lot we are, English schoolboys need little excuse to start bullying younger children and John was a sitting target. Not only did he look like a sweet little mama's boy, but he was still wearing shorts while most of the other boys were proudly showing off their long trousers. And then, of course, there was big brother David.

'I was done for as soon as I got there because of him,' John says, still with a hint of despair in his voice at the hopelessness of the situation. 'Not only did I get bullied by the boys for the way I looked but the teachers were after me too. They just wanted to get at me because they couldn't get anywhere with him. David defied them. They'd threaten him with all kinds of punishment and he didn't care. He'd just stand up to them and fight back. There was this English teacher who was basically a swine and he hated David because David answered back. So he sent me to see the headmaster almost before I'd got through the door! I hadn't done anything wrong. I hadn't done anything. I hadn't had time! And so there I was, this pathetic little kid, scared to death in the headmaster's study staring at this cupboard full of canes. He didn't use any of them that time but I got it later. Never as often as David, though.'

Part of John's problem at school was that David had broken with tradition and gone to Southend High School instead of

Westcliffe where almost everyone from their primary school went. He made the switch because they played rugby at Westcliff and David was a mad keen footballer. So, after he passed his eleven-plus, brother John followed in his footsteps, even more lonely than he would have felt under normal circumstances because all his chums had moved on to Westcliff.

The reception he got, both from masters and pupils, turned John off school for good. 'Basically, my reaction was "Well, if you're going to be like that, screw you!" which was really stupid on my part because you are the only one that really suffers. I probably wouldn't have been a brilliant student under any circumstances, but that took care of any chance I had of doing anything great.'

How great a tennis player John Lloyd could have become, had he possessed his older brother's obsessive desire to wring the last drop of juice from life and any talent God had given him, will never be known. But it remains a source of considerable frustration to John Barrett, Roger Becker and various other people involved with British tennis during the Seventies. Unlike David, John was a complete natural, blessed with all the easy fluency of shotmaking that only the finest racket players possess. But John was never driven. Worse than that, he was lazy. If he hadn't been born into a sports-mad family where tennis was simply an unavoidable way of life, John would have become the country's leading couch potato, racking up more hours in front of a television set than anyone alive. 'John was so transfixed by it he would watch the spot go out,' says his great friend Peter Risdon who had helped the younger Lloyd's career by sending him down to Lew Hoad's Campo de Tenis on the Costa del Sol for some personal coaching from the great Wimbledon champion. It wasn't that he didn't like tennis. He loved all sports and watched them avidly but, especially in his youth, he was simply too damned idle to get out in less than comfortable weather — which means 90 per cent of the year if you live near the North Sea — and practise. Matches motivated him and he never shirked his duty for Britain, but the contrast between his attitude and that of his first wife was clearly reflected by their respective achievements on court. Chris Evert won everything several times over while John won very little.

'He can't be termed a success because he didn't maximise his talent,' says David, saying nothing that he hasn't said to John's face.

'Can't argue with that,' John admits. 'There were times when I could have worked harder.'

Roger Becker, the most famous Becker in tennis until a certain red-headed German started winning Wimbledon at seventeen, had a long relationship with British Davis Cup teams through the Sixties and Seventies as both team and personal coach to many of the players. He discovered the contrast between John and Chrissie one week at Queen's when they were both practising in London in preparation for the French Open. Obviously that meant they were playing on the dusty clay courts and conditions were not very pleasant when Roger took John out for a hit one morning.

'We hadn't been out there fifteen minutes when John started complaining about the wind and how the red dust was getting into his hair,' Becker recalls. 'It was useless trying to go on. He just wasn't into it. The next day the weather was still foul but Chris needed to practise and so we went out, again in a nasty wind, and she never said a word. Just got on with it.'

John McEnroe and Monolo Santana were lousy practice players, too, but the sad thing about John Lloyd's career was that he was just one notch below being able to get away with it.

'I coached the Spanish Davis Cup team for a while and Santana had this amazing record,' said Becker. 'Absolutely brilliant. But hopeless on the practice court. Wasn't even worth trying to get started. You just had to let him go out and play and such was his ability that he never let you down.'

Unfortunately John Lloyd was never quite that good although it must be remembered that he did reach a Grand Slam Final — the first British player to do so since Fred Perry in the Thirties — even though it was at Kooyong during those years when the Australian Open did not attract all the world's best players. Nevertheless, he beat John Newcombe, only just past his peak, in the quarter-final and then went down in five sets to Vitas Gerulaitis in the final, which was no disgrace. That same year, 1977, he also reached the final of the Swiss Indoors in Basle and the Benson & Hedges Championships at Wembley which, in those days, was one of the premier indoor events in the world. Again, he could hardly have been expected to win either event as the man who beat him in both finals was called Bjorn Borg, then at the height of his powers. But at Wembley, John had demonstrated just what kind of a threat he could have become to the world's top players by knocking off his Davis Cup team mate, Mark Cox, who was then the British No. 1, in the second round, Brian Gottfried in straight sets in the quarters, and Gottfried's long-time doubles partner, Raul Ramirez, in the semis.

So what happened? Well, to be glib about it, I suppose Chrissie happened. It was hard work getting to all those finals and, if he was to maintain that level, he would have needed to concentrate 100 per cent on his own game. That means leading a selfish existence that forces everyone around you to dovetail their lives with yours. Chris, to her credit, supported him as best she could and often spent time at tournaments with John, but the men's and women's tours were already divided which meant that, had they both played full-time, they would only have seen each other at Grand Slams. Something had to give. After they announced their engagement in December 1978, following a year of furtive courtship, John, being the sweet-natured kind of guy he is, allowed his future wife's career to take precedence and it was only after their first break-up that he became a serious threat in singles again. By that time Bob Brett, the Australian coach who was already making a name for himself as the most intelligent of his breed on the tour, had introduced John to Stan Nicholes, the former Australian Olympic weight-lifting champion who had been trainer to most of Harry Hopman's great Australian Davis Cup teams during the years of Frank Sedgman, Lew Hoad and Rod Laver. John had been having continuous problems with his racket arm, but they disappeared after several sessions at Nicholes's Melbourne gym where he built up protective muscle on the arm and generally made Lloyd far stronger in the upper body. John was still on speaking terms with his wife and Chris, realising that she needed extra physical strength to keep pace with her nutrition-driven rival Martina Navratilova, also benefited from Nicholes's expertise. John was soon working full-time with Brett who had also agreed to help Paul McNamee, another player trying to reconstruct a career relatively late in life.

Both players benefited from Brett's guidance, but it was John who made the most dramatic impact when he scored great victories over Peter Fleming and Johan Kriek to reach the quarter-final of the US Open in 1983. He even pushed Jimmy Connors hard in the first set of his next match before being overwhelmed as much by Connors's personality as his shot making. Once again one was left to ponder what might have been if John had been blessed with just a little of David's cussed character that made it impossible for him to be intimidated by anyone.

'John could have done better against Jimmy that year but he had played really well up till then,' Brett recalls. 'Helping him to get back to his best ever ranking of 21 in the world was very satisfying for me and nothing more than he deserved because he had worked very hard during that period.'

It was around that time, in 1983 and '84, that John landed his two Wimbledon mixed doubles titles in partnership with the little Australian, affectionately known as 'Rabbit', Wendy Turnbull. Again, there are those who will say that this is a secondary achievement for a man of such ability, but there are many fine players of both sexes who have never got their hands on a Wimbledon title of any description and it is not the players' fault that the mixed is given such short thrift. I am one of those who are convinced that, properly presented, a World Mixed Doubles Championship would have enormous spectator appeal providing a good selection of the top names participated.

At any rate, it was a sphere of the game in which John excelled. His personality was well suited to doubles and his ability to get on with people — once he had escaped from Southend High School — only served to make his path through life even smoother. It says much for him and the entire Lloyd family that there seems to have been almost no unpleasant sibling rivalry between the brothers despite the fact that they were all destined to take up the same awkwardly competitive and individualistic sport that demands more than the average ration of ego.

If they ever had to play each other in tournaments, the memory seems to have been effectively blocked from the mind which, as any psychologist will tell you, means the experience was not a pleasant one.

'I honestly can't remember if I've ever played David in singles,' John says. 'I know I have in doubles but I suppose I must have played him in singles somewhere. I know I've never beaten him. I played Tony when we were younger and we both hated every second of it. It was just a bad situation. We have always been very supportive of each other and, David being six years older than me, there was a good gap. I caught up with him as a player at around seventeen or eighteen when he was already in his twenties, but I can't say I ever wanted to beat him, just like I never wanted to beat my father, and Tony never wanted to beat me. It was just the way we felt about each other.'

But John has not forgotten his first trip to somewhere a little more foreign than France or Spain, places he quickly became familiar with once Barrett had taken charge of his coaching. 'I went to Egypt and it was a disastrous trip. I had to fly on my own and, after fourteen hours, with all sorts of delays, the plane landed at four o'clock in the morning. There was no one to pick me up and I had no idea which hotel I was staying at. You can imagine what a panic I was in. So the first guy I found who spoke English agreed to help and we set off, stopping at about fifteen hotels before we found the right one. David came in two days later. We were playing in a sort of nation's cup tournament and we were up against the Soviets. They had a huge bloke called something like Korotkov and another little squat one with bulging muscles and, sure enough, David got into an argument with the big one up at the net. I was the size of an insect at the time and I started imagining what kind of a mess we'd be in if it came to fisticuffs. It didn't thank goodness, but no doubt David would have looked after me. He was always tremendously supportive.'

John was reminiscing on the comfortable settee at his prettily decorated house in Pacific Palisades, California where he has set up home with his second wife, Deborah, and their two children, Aidan and Hayley. The contrast with John's old bachelor flat in Wimbledon is stark. Debbie's influence is everywhere, with the floral theme of the colourfully co-ordinated interior matched by the abundance of flowers in the front garden. The village of Pacific Palisades sits almost at the end of Sunset Boulevard, a winding road that stretches far beyond the area of the famous Strip in West Hollywood. It takes you, in fact, all the way down to the Pacific Ocean, and it is a couple of miles before the beach that the Lloyd's pale blue two-storey home sits on a quiet suburban street just off Sunset.

One senses that John, with a family to support, is more motivated to get up off that sofa today than he might have been in the past. During his marriage to Chris, he had enjoyed the role of husband, helper and chief supporter to a superstar for a time but, after the break-up, it did not take him long to realise that he was far better suited to the kind of stable, loving relationship Deborah offers him, out of the limelight.

Now, although he refuses the easy pickings that are available to anyone of his talent and celebrity who is prepared to coach film stars and studio tycoons around Hollywood, he does get involved in corporate clinics and exhibition matches through his work for Grand Slams Sports, a company formed by Fred Stolle and Cliff Drysdale in which he and eleven others, including Ken Rosewall and Roy Emerson, have a direct stake. He also takes very seriously his new career on Jimmy Connors's Grand Champions Tour which has become increasingly successful and lucrative for the participants in the last couple of years. He relishes the competition now and, unlike some people, has always got on well with Connors. Perhaps their mutual link to Chris Evert, to whom Jimmy was engaged before she married John, has something to do with it.

John also plays regularly on the ATP Senior Tour and his desire to grab the opportunities that are still available late in his career was readily evident a few years ago when the Seniors were playing at the ATP Tour headquarters at Ponte Vedra Beach, Florida. John had flown in from somewhere with a bad cold and, after a restless night, had gone to see the doctor on the morning the tournament was due to begin. The doctor diagnosed pneumonia and told him to go straight to bed.

'No tennis for you this week,' he said firmly.

'But you don't understand,' replied John incredulously. 'I'm playing doubles with Rod Laver! I've waited years and years to get the chance to play with Rod and nothing's going to stop me now.'

And nothing did. Pumped full of antibiotics, John got himself out on court and performed creditably before he and Laver lost to Ken Rosewall and Tom Gullikson. David would have been proud of him.

Chapter 3

Davis Cup

When he is with his parents, David Lloyd will occasionally pull out a copy of the tape of a Davis Cup match played on Wimbledon's No. 1 Court in 1978. Nobody who was there to witness it will need to be reminded what it shows. 'It's amazing to watch it after all these years and think, Did I really do that?' he says.

Well, he did do that which, translated, means that he took a Davis Cup doubles by the scruff of the neck and, in one of the most inspirationally brilliant individual performances I have ever seen on a doubles court, turned a match inside out and enabled Britain to keep the tie against Italy alive after they had been trailing by two sets to love.

Paul McNamee, one of the few doubles experts capable of rivalling David's jack-in-the-box intensity and athleticism, was the only other player I saw offer a comparable sort of performance in Davis Cup when he and Mark Edmondson defeated Anders Jarryd and Hans Simonsson in the Australia v. Sweden Final of 1983 at Kooyong. But on that occasion it was a question of one man's dynamism crushing the opposition from the word go. The Aussies, who went on to win the Cup, won the doubles in three devastating sets that rarely saw McNamee's feet touch the ground as he flung himself about at the net.

At Wimbledon five years earlier, Britain were in a very different situation. Although the fast grass of No. 1 Court was supposed to work in the home side's favour, the Italians, raucously supported by nearly 5,000 of their companions, had got away to a fast start on the first day with Tonino Zugarelli surprising Roger Taylor with his grass court dexterity to win 6–1 in the fourth, and Adriano Panatta, whose big serve and more than adequate volley equipped him

39

perfectly for grass, had survived a long struggle with John Lloyd to win 6–4 in the fifth. So Britain were two–nil down which surprised the critical coterie of British tennis writers which in those days included such stalwarts of the art as Lance Tingay of the *Daily Telegraph*, Frank Rostron of the *Daily Express* and Laurie Pignon of the *Daily Mail*. They had watched this British team, captained by Paul Hutchins, dismiss a strong French squad 4–1 at Eastbourne with the kind of authority British players should be expected to produce on grass; and the Lloyd brothers putting the tie beyond France's grasp by beating François Jauffret and Patrick Proisy in four well-played sets.

The Italians were stronger, not solely because of Panatta's stature as a world-class player but because he was partnered in doubles by one of the greatest talents European tennis has produced since World War II. His results will refute such an accolade because Paolo Bertolucci was too indolent to go through the nasty machinations of winning more than was absolutely necessary. Even so, he couldn't help winning the odd tournament like the German Open in Hamburg while making everyone else look slightly second-class.

Bertolucci would give you a speech on his lack of achievement any time you asked. 'Panatta — he is No. 1. I am very happy for him. Everybody follow him around and I can go to the beach and nobody notice. I enjoy to play and make beautiful shots. For me, is more important to make beautiful shot than to win the match. If I hit nice backhand down line, just how I want it, I am happy. It is enough.'

With this philosophy, it was hardly surprising that Bertolucci only really came alive when Panatta was there to kick-start his motor and make sure that his stubby little legs moved as fast as they were able. They had been moving pretty well in the previous round when he and Panatta scored a surprisingly decisive straight set victory in Bologna over the talented Yugoslav duo Nikki Pilic and Zeljko Franulovic and, as the match got under way at Wimbledon, there was every indication that this was going to be another vintage performance.

Most Italian restaurants in London were, presumably, either closed or desperately short-staffed, because another startlingly large contingent of Italian supporters were in place to see Panatta and Bertolucci move inexorably towards clinching the tie by taking the first two sets 8–6, 6–3. There had been flashes of excitement — Panatta's winning forehand on set point in the first set hit in the act of falling backwards over the baseline was one of them — but there was little, as Rex Bellamy put it in the following day's *Times*, 'to distress the pulse rate'.

Then, suddenly, the match underwent a scarcely perceptible change, as matches sometimes do. The experienced observer senses it almost before anything concrete has happened, like a dog feeling the on-coming earthquake through its sensitive paws before a mere human has any inkling of impending disaster. Possibly the Italians relaxed their grip a little as teams can when they have two sets in their pocket. Panatta, with his air of casual arrogance — so impressive when things were going his way, so infuriating when they were not — pushed at a forehand half-volley that flew an inch out of court. The Italian fans didn't like the call but it stood and Britain had broken for 5–3. David Lloyd who, at changeovers, had never let his brother forget that the match was far from over, served out for the set.

Redoubling his efforts, David initiated a break in the first game of the fourth and although Italy broke back, some fine returns from John created a third game against the serve and once again David found himself serving for the set. But this time it was not so easy. He had three set points and the Italians five break back points but, after seven deuces had sent the atmosphere soaring to fever pitch, Panatta and Bertolucci managed to clinch it and so began a long sequence in which they were always the odd game up. Under those circumstances, it is never fun to be the team that is behind because every break point is a match point and that can be terrible for the nerves.

'But defeat never seemed to enter David's head,' said John, still smiling at the memory all those years later. 'I had felt a bit flat at first. I didn't seem to have much zip. Even so I thought we should have been one set all. But I was never allowed to get defeatist. He kept on telling me, "Come on, come on, we can do this!" He was very aggressive, almost physical with me. And eventually I started to believe him. You had to. His belief was so unquestioning, so definite.'

It needed to be because the Lloyds had their backs to the wall time and again as the drama unfolded, enveloping No. 1 in a cacophony of sound, rising and falling with every shot played, every opportunity missed. At 9–10, drawing on fraternal courage, John saved a match point with nothing less hazardous than a drive volley. At 14–15, the Italians reached four more match points but were thwarted by David at every turn, throwing himself this way and that at the net.

And then, seemingly out of nowhere, the opportunity was Britain's and John secured the break for 17–16 with a backhand volley. Ecstatic, an elderly lady stood up and waved Union Jacks in both hands. Could David do it again? Absolutely. No question — not even after Bertolucci had conjured a magical half-volley to give the Italians a chance of a break back. David shrugged that off and served out to level the match at two sets all.

Bertolucci, in his charmingly vague way, focused his memory on the match when I asked him about it during the Monte Carlo Open this year. 'Ah yes, I remember,' he said. 'Forehands. Forehand service returns. Fantastic. Was that John playing in the right hand court? No? David? Ah well, then, it was David. He returned fantastic.'

Both brothers had been playing well but there was no question as to who was playing 'fantastic'. David had been the motivator; the pint-sized human dynamo who had continually thrown himself into the path of Italian returns, defying them to pass him, bloody-mindedly refusing to give up. But now, as Rex Bellamy observed in his inimitable style, he simply got better.

'Now he played as if, for twenty-two minutes that he will remember until he dies, he thought he was the greatest player who ever lived. The man had been working himself into the ground for three hours and a half. But now he actually accelerated. He broke a racket. He was running, leaping, lunging, hurtling about like a racing car that had gone out of control. But David Lloyd had not gone out of control. He knew what he was doing and, of the four tired men, it was David Lloyd, restored to the team last month for the first time since 1974, who had the reserves of energy and inspiration to blast Britain through the breach that fourth set had created. With that the Italians were cooked physically and mentally. Today, they will remember yesterday.'

So wrote Bellamy for the readers of *The Times* and the last sentence reminds us that this was still an age when big-time sport was not played on Sundays in Britain. Bellamy did not write for *The Sunday Times* so 'today' had to be the final day of the tie, a Saturday, the doubles having taken place on a Friday. Whatever day of the week, it was, indeed, a day David will never forget for it proved what the spirit can achieve in forcing the body into feats normally beyond its reach. Physically, Lloyd's performance was extraordinary enough in the way he flung himself about the net, but it was the force of his personality that I shall always remember — that driving, hair-raising will to win that left his opponents stunned. Tennis matches can be won by personality as Boris Becker demonstrated in the 1995 Wimbledon semi-final against Andre Agassi. The American, with the first set safely tucked away, was seemingly on course for another victory over the man he had beaten so regularly, when he was suddenly stopped dead in his tracks. It was as if Boris had reached across the net and grabbed Andre by the throat, yelling, 'No! You're NOT going to do this to me again. This is MY court!' And then proceeded to match his wrathful indignation with a performance that became increasingly inspirational.

That, in essence, was what David Lloyd achieved on No. 1 Court that Friday afternoon in 1978, and Rex was right. He will never forget it.

Davis Cup was not always a triumph for David, although there was certainly no shortage of memorable moments, some of them bordering on the notorious. A year later, Britain had to travel to Bucharest for a European Zone A semi-final. It was a formidable task, for the dreaded pair of Ion Tiriac and Ilie Nastase, although just past their peak, were still capable of playing some extraordinary tennis. Neither was likely to create quite as much mayhem as they had during the unforgettable Davis Cup Final against Dennis Ralston's United States team in 1972 which Stan Smith somehow managed to win for the visitors, but, nonetheless, the odds on a

Davis Cup tie passing without incident in Bucharest are never very good. And they verge on the ridiculous if you have two personalities like Nastase and David Lloyd in opposite teams. They simply become lightning rods for disaster.

But there was, as usual, a calm before the storm. On Friday, June 10, Britain battled through a hot and humid afternoon at the Progresul Club and ended up two rubbers down. That came as a disappointment to the young British captain, Paul Hutchins, who had expected that his No. 1 singles player, John Lloyd, would defeat the inexperienced Romanian No. 2, Dmitru Haradau. When Lloyd won the first set 6–2, there seemed every chance that he would. But Haradau proved himself a powerful and determined competitor, and when Lloyd started to get cramp in his racket hand, the match slid away from him.

In the opening singles, John Feaver had performed creditably against Nastase in his first ever Davis Cup rubber. Like all players who suffer from periodic neurosis about various aspects of their game — which is 98 per cent of pros on the tour — Feaver had, at that time, lost confidence in his serve. As the big West Countryman has one of the deadliest first serves in tennis, it was a considerable handicap to go into a match against Nastase in Bucharest with one's best shot on crutches. But when John started slicing his first serve instead of hitting it hard and flat, there was no doubt that it was in need of mental, if not physical, repair. Yet even without that potent weapon, Feaver showed a surprising aptitude for sticking to it on slow clay and, after winning the third set, he led 4–2 in the fourth before Ilie capitalised on a few English errors and ran it out 6–4.

The day's play had presented few problems for the experienced Spanish referee, Jaime Bartroli. The line calling had been above average and, to the occasional surprise of the large crowd, what few dubious calls there were tended to be in favour of Britain. And from the point of view of clashing personalities, there was no problem between Nastase and Feaver. They had played doubles together once on the US Indoor Circuit and had always got along.

But the next day the players on court produced very different vibes. In their playing days, Ilie Nastase and David Lloyd should never have been separated by anything as frail and inadequate as a tennis net. A concrete wall perhaps, or, if they insisted on being able to see each other, bullet-proof glass might suffice; but nothing which allowed their high voltage nerve ends to rub themselves raw. With two people who basically found each other irritating, it was only a question of time before the sparks created an almighty explosion.

On this occasion it took a little over an hour. Nastase and Tiriac had won the first set 9–7 and the Lloyds were leading 2–0 in the second when David Lloyd chased a wide ball at such speed that he ended up on the Romanians' side of the net. As fate would have it, David and Ilie were in the net positions as John Lloyd prepared to serve the next point, so verbal contact became all too easy.

Nastase began making some funny and relatively harmless remark about David trespassing on Romanian territory. Whether David heard what Nastase said correctly or not is a moot point. What is clear is that he had been waiting for Nastase to make a wrong move. And at the first suggestion of it, Lloyd, bristling visibly, pounced.

'What was that you said?' David snapped back, cocking his head in Nastase's direction. Even from the stands, his whole stance, expression and attitude seemed provocative, and from a distance of five feet across the net there was no way that Ilie was going to have enough self-control or sense to resist what seemed to him to be a challenge.

So he replied with a phrase that was rather more colourful. David heard that clearly enough and, still not satisfied that he had hooked his fish, said, 'What was that? I didn't hear.'

Nastase was probably quite well aware of what he was letting himself in for, but there is something in his character which will not allow him to back away, even if the bait is clearly marked 'DANGER — DON'T TOUCH'. So once again he repeated the insult and Lloyd had got him.

'That's it, that's it,' David shouted in a fit of moral indignation. 'I'm not taking any more of that.' And he strode off court. The crowd, who had heard nothing of the conversation at the net, were momentarily stunned, but quickly added their own cacophony of boos and whistles to a state of total confusion which had erupted on court.

At first David said he was going to quit in protest. Then in quick succession, David and Ilie started to walk towards each other gesticulating; Tiriac and Bartroli got between them; Nastase tried to tap Lloyd over the head (David later maintained that Ilie hit him with his racket); Paul Hutchins tried to talk to Bartroli; the British coach, Roger Becker, raced down out of the players' enclosure to have a soothing word with David who had been frog-marched backwards off court by Bartroli and Constantin Nastase, the Romanian captain; and up in his chair the umpire made vain attempts to attract somebody's attention. Only John Lloyd stayed on his side of the net, aloof from the chaos.

After a full ten-minute hiatus, Bartroli got everyone back on court and publicly warned Nastase for insulting behaviour. The line calling continued to be generally good and even the British players acknowledged later that Tiriac had been excellent throughout, never disputing a call and once even signalling a dubious decision in Britain's favour. Tiriac seemed to be enjoying his role as the elder statesman in this tie. With much shaking of his curly head and shrugging of the shoulders, he adopted a gently superior air to any dispute that arose, as if admonishing little kiddies for getting up to such childish games.

But even Tiriac in this benign mood could not prevent further arguments from flaring up as the match progressed. The score had reached 8–7 to Romania in the fourth set when Bartroli changed a call in Britain's favour, thus making John Lloyd 15–30 down on his serve instead of facing three match points. Then it started to rain in earnest. Obviously the Romanians wanted to continue and just as obviously, Hutchins wanted to get his team off court. Anything to break a spell when it is going against you. Once again David Lloyd was the most visible advocate for stopping, and when Bartroli finally decided to call the players off, David, swathed in a huge towel that made him look like a senator in ancient Rome, gave the hissing crowd a deep facetious bow and marched out of the arena.

In the corridor leading to the locker room, Nastase confronted Hutchins. 'You running this match, Mr Hutchins?' Ilie asked coldly. 'Or perhaps David Lloyd is?' 'It's the referee's decision,' Hutchins replied.

When the match resumed, David netted a forehand volley; John hit a smash out of court; and Romania had gained an unassailable 3–0 lead in the tie. But the drama was not over.

That evening an extraordinary dinner took place in the large restaurant of the Inter-Continental Hotel. The hotel was evidently not very busy that weekend for the British team virtually had the place to themselves. A group of Africans occupied one nearby table and, over in a far corner, John Parsons, then writing for the *Daily Mail*, entertained Christopher Bullock, the chairman of the LTA, to dinner.

Hutchins's team were seated at a large circular table in the middle of the room. Apart from the Lloyds and John Feaver, the party included Roger Becker and Richard Lewis, who has since risen to a position of power in the LTA hierarchy.

Evidently Hutchins had been at a series of meetings after the end of the match, both with members of his team and with Jaime Bartroli, but none seemed to have helped to alleviate the feeling of acute disappointment and nervous tension that still pervaded the group. And one major and quite startling suggestion remained unresolved: a move was afoot for the British team to pack their bags and leave without completing the remaining two rubbers, as both Davis Cup rules and sporting etiquette demanded. It was David Lloyd who was advocating this drastic action, and he was supported by Becker.

'Even if there's a small chance of doing some good, it would be worth it,' said David. 'Sometime, somewhere, someone's just got to take a stand against Nastase's type of behaviour and we have a golden opportunity to do it right now. How is anyone ever going to be able to persuade kids that Nastase's antics are not the proper way to behave on a tennis court if we go on condoning it?'

'But we've lost,' Feaver interjected. 'It would look like sour grapes.'

'Quite apart from that, we've got a problem with Bartroli,' Hutchins added. 'He says he never heard Ilie make those remarks to David and never saw David being hit over the head with a racket. He feels that in the circumstances, he cannot put those incidents in his report to the ITF. So without evidence from the referee to back our action, I think we'd risk having ourselves banned from the Davis Cup next year.'

'Then it's not worth it,' said John Lloyd. 'British tennis would lose and the Romanians would get off free. What would be the point in that?'

Becker shook his head. 'I tend to agree with David. No matter what the consequences, I just think it is time someone took a stand.'

'That's right,' said David vehemently. 'You guys can do what you want, but I'm on that early flight in the morning no matter what.'

'How can you leave the team now?' Lewis shot back heatedly. 'We've worked as a team, trained as a team, played as a team and we should stick it out as a team. How can you bugger off now just because you're upset?'

'Well, I'm sorry but I'm going and that's that,' David replied. 'If you're gutless enough not to come to a decision either way, I can't help it.'

'Well, I wish you'd go right now,' Lewis retorted, his fair features suddenly turning crimson with rage. 'And if you're going to call me gutless, you can step outside and we'll discover who's gutless. No one's ever called me that before.'

If honour and moral behaviour are close relations, then one could argue, somewhat ironically, that it was David's complaint about the lowering of the standard of behaviour which had created the row in the first place.

Even so, the elder Lloyd had to keep a very firm grip on himself to avoid getting dragged into a brawl. For Lewis suddenly slammed down his soup spoon, jumped up and grabbed David by the collar, twisting it in a large fist in an effort to yank him to his feet. Refusing to react, David stared down at his plate and said nothing. Everyone round the table froze in a mixture of shock and embarrassment. The French-speaking Africans at the next table were the first to react.

'Eh, doucement, mon ami,' one of them said.

'Oh, shut up,' snarled Lewis, who eventually responded to the more recognisable tones of his captain and his coach by resuming his seat.

'Bloody idiots,' someone muttered as the Africans cracked jokes about what to them must have seemed an amusing scene.

'I think,' said Feaver, 'they would have more right to call us idiots.'

'Look, try and calm down,' Hutchins interjected. 'We're all uptight and it's getting to us.'

'You mean, he's got to us,' replied Lewis who was slowly returning to his normal colour. 'Bloody Nastase's the one who got through to us.'

And of course Richard Lewis was right. With one obscene and insulting phrase repeated twice across a net, Nastase had set friend against friend and temporarily disrupted the excellent team spirit — so eloquently voiced by Lewis in his moment of anger — that Hutchins had carefully nurtured. That was much more than Ilie had intended, if, indeed, he had intended anything. Having had the red rag waved in his face, he had simply unsheathed his horns and gored. The wounds, as usual, had run deep.

If any player but David Lloyd had been on the other side of that net, it would probably never have happened. (But Kipling did not write 'If' with Nastase in mind. 'If you can keep your head when all about you are losing theirs and blaming it on you . . .' No, no — Ilie can never be counted on to handle stuff like that.)

But there weren't many question marks left when this particular situation had run its course. After a long, heart-searching talk with Hutchins after dinner, David Lloyd reluctantly agreed to stay with the team. But when the ITF pronounced judgement several months later after reading Bartroli's report, David was partially vindicated even though he did not escape mild censure himself. For the International Federation decided to get tough with Ilie and banned him from all Davis Cup play in 1978 — Bartroli having finally decided to back up Hutchins's sweeping condemnation of Nastase's behaviour in his own report. The Spanish referee did, however, point out that Lloyd himself had acted in a provocative manner. It was a fair judgement.

The following year was the most satisfying — and surprising — for Britain in Davis Cup play since the halcyon days of Fred Perry and Bunny Austin in the mid-Thirties. Against considerable odds, Britain went all the way to the final; all the way, in fact, to the still unfinished Mission Hills Country Club at Rancho Mirage, California. The Lloyd family, who were there in force for the occasion, liked what they saw and it was very soon afterwards that John bought a house from the South African, Ray Moore, just down Frank Sinatra Drive at Sunrise.

The route to California had been strewn with pitfalls that lesser British teams might not have survived. After a routine dismissal of Monaco in the Principality, Austria were also crushed 5–0, this time on the grass courts at Bristol. The semi-final of the European Zone Group A was, however, altogether more formidable. It required a trip to Paris and the daunting clay courts of Roland Garros. Perry might have triumphed there, but since the war only Mike Sangster, who had utilised his massive serve to earn himself a semi-final place in the French Championships in the Sixties, had returned from Paris with anything but dust on his shoes and despair in his heart.

But Paul Hutchins, on this occasion, knew that there was a window of opportunity for his team that could be exploited. The French were in a state of transition. François Jauffret, a clay court master, was still able to play doubles, but the singles duties were entrusted to the inexperienced Eric Deblicker and the lanky young giant Arthur Ashe had plucked from Africa five years before called Yannick Noah. The man who would help carry France on a wave of tennis mania into the Eighties and send the nation into paroxysms of joy by winning the French title in 1983, was still a colt when the British team arrived in Paris and, although of similar age, Buster Mottram was already a more cunning competitor. The son of the former British No. 1 Tony Mottram came through to beat Noah in four sets, and John Lloyd followed up with one of his most courageous performances on clay to beat Deblicker in five.

With Jauffret to guide him, Noah was too much of a handful for the Lloyd brothers in doubles and the French won in straight sets, but Mottram quickly settled the issue by defeating Deblicker in three. For Britain to return triumphant from such a testing Davis Cup excursion on continental clay was almost as rare as champagne without the bubbles, but everything had to be put on ice until Czechoslovakia were dealt with in the Zone Final on the smooth grass courts of Devonshire Park, Eastbourne. Again, the timing was perfect for Britain. Jan Kodes, who had proved himself a seriously competitive grass court player, not merely by winning Wimbledon in the boycott year of 1973 but by reaching two Forest Hills finals, was past his best, and Ivan Lendl was nothing more than a stringy youth of high promise.

As a result Britain's battle-hardened team swept through the tie in style after John Lloyd proved once again that he had plenty of his brother's fighting spirit when the occasion demanded by winning a cliff-hanger against the talented but slightly demented Jiri Hrebec 12–10 in the fifth. Mottram then beat Lendl in straight sets and David Lloyd, given the left-handed Mark Cox as a partner on this occasion, eventually quelled the dogged resistance put up by Kodes and Tomas Smid to win 6–4 in the fifth.

When the whole thing was wrapped up 5–0, Britain had played four ties for the loss of only two rubbers, an amazing performance for a team without a single representative ranked in the world's top twenty. John Lloyd's ATP ranking that year hovered in the twenties, while Mottram was marginally lower. Cox had been a stalwart of the great World Championship Tennis tour groups in the early Seventies but was slipping by this time, and David Lloyd's singles rating never cracked the top one hundred.

But the players were functioning as a unit and, although Mottram had eccentric tendencies, Hutchins's low-key style of leadership seemed to be sufficient to allow everyone to play at their maximum. They needed to because the Davis Cup campaign was a harder slog in those days with zonal groups to fight through before the Inter Zone Finals which would be the equivalent of World Group semi-finals today. And, of course, by that stage nothing got any easier.

Britain's next opponents were none other than Australia, the country synonymous with Davis Cup glory in the legendary days of Harry Hopman. Again the British needed a little help from fate and the passage of time and they got both. Davis Cup venues are decided on where the two teams last met and as Britain had travelled to Australia on the previous occasion, Hutchins had the choice of venue and chose a one-off location for Davis Cup indoors at Crystal Palace in London. The other piece of good fortune was that Hopman had retired as Davis Cup captain several years before and, as a result, Australia's rich seam of tennis talent was no longer being mined.

However Neale Fraser was not exactly scraping the barrel when he arrived in London in the autumn of 1978. He had Tony Roche, one of the last of Hopman's protégés, to play singles with the best of the next generation, John Alexander. Both were experienced Davis Cup campaigners, and if Roche was better known as a doubles player, his singles record was also one that would make most players green with envy — French Open Champion and finalist at Wimbledon and Forest Hills. Roche could have played doubles as well, of course, but not surprisingly Fraser decided to opt for a recognised team in Ross Case and Geoff Masters who were good enough to win Wimbledon in 1977.

So Britain's task was formidable but, once again, they rose to the occasion and, after getting off to a flyer with Mottram beating Roche in four sets and John Lloyd trouncing Alexander in three, stunned themselves as well as everyone else by wrapping up a place in the final in two days. David Lloyd and Cox grabbed the opportunity to put the tie beyond Australia's reach by beating Case and Masters 6–3 in the fourth.

'That was my most satisfying Davis Cup performance,' David recalled. 'Beating the Aussies is always special and getting to the final was just a tremendous bonus.'

Although they did not realise it at the time, any faint hope Britain had of pulling off the ultimate upset and beating the United States in California vanished when a freckle-faced, tousled-haired teenager called John McEnroe was nominated for his Davis Cup singles debut. Arthur Ashe and Vitas Gerulaitis had played singles against Sweden in Gothenberg in the previous round but neither was available for the final. Ashe had succumbed to the pain caused by a spur on his heel which had been troubling him for some time, and Gerulaitis was a mercurial performer capable of great highs and lows. Both might have been more susceptible to the twin talents of Mottram and John Lloyd than McEnroe who made an astonishing entry in the annals of Davis Cup history by slaughtering Lloyd 6–1, 6–2, 6–2 and in the first of the reverse singles Mottram, Britain's first-day hero, 6–2, 6–2, 6–1.

'I've been beaten badly by people but no one has ever made me feel a complete fool on a tennis court like McEnroe did today,' admitted John afterwards. He was not the first player to feel that way as McEnroe went on to compile the best record of any American player in Davis Cup history, notching up a total of 69 victories in singles and doubles.

On this occasion he was not called upon to play doubles because the captain, Tony Trabert, was more than satisfied that Stan Smith and Bob Lutz could do the job and he was not wrong. Trabert remembers it well. The bulky, diamond-studded ring that was given to the players and their captain as a momento of that year's successful Davis Cup campaign was still on Trabert's finger when he told me about the tactics he had employed as we chatted in the press room at this year's German Open in Hamburg.

'I wanted Stan and Bob to keep moving out there because, like me, they are both big men and I know from experience that you can get a bit static in doubles if you don't keep really active at the net,' said Trabert. 'So I told them both to poach at every opportunity and try to put extra pressure on the Brits by cutting out the cross court service return. It worked really well in the first set and I told them to just keep doing it if the opposition changed tactics and tried to go down the line. But, for some reason, they never did. Maybe they weren't confident on that shot or something, but they kept going cross court and our guys had a field day poaching those returns.'

Tactically, it was even more of a mismatch than it should have been on court because the playing records of Trabert and Hutchins did not bear comparison. Hutchins had done well with a team that needed his kind of quiet, nice-guy calmness to handle some pretty volatile personalities — Cox and Mottram rarely saw eye to eye on anything from tennis to politics — but his own experience in the big theatre of top-flight Davis Cup play was non-existent when matched up against the American who had helped the United States recover the Cup from Australia in front of what Tony remembers as a 26,000 crowd (some record books may say a couple of thousand more) at White City in Sydney in 1955, the same year he ruled the tennis world by winning the three biggest Grand Slams at

Wimbledon, Roland Garros and Forest Hills. He was one of the great winners of all time, and he had at his disposal a couple of players in Smith and Lutz who will go down as one of the most effective doubles combinations of their era. David Lloyd tried his damnedest as usual and Cox came up with a few heavy left-handed blows, but there was no hiding the gap in class and the Americans won in straight sets to give the US a 2–1 lead.

Many had expected that it would be all over by then because Mottram did not start favourite to beat Brian Gottfried in the second singles. Gottfried, who may have spent more time on a practice court than any other player alive, had been in the French Open final a couple of years before and was, if anything, even more comfortable on the hard cement-style courts being used at Mission Hills, a sprawling luxury resort, originally owned by Colgate whose CEO at the time, David Foster, was a tennis fanatic. Once the golf course had been built, Foster initiated the opening of the tennis centre and appointed the former Wimbledon finalist Dennis Ralston as a high-profile Director of Tennis. By 1978, Mission Hills was becoming a major venue for professional events and, in the space of a few months, hosted the men's American Airlines Tennis Games, the women's year-end Championships and the Davis Cup Final.

The second singles began in the warm December sunshine with Gottfried dominating the first two sets. Then, as the desert temperatures plummeted, Mottram began a remarkable fight-back as the local residents headed home for dinner. By the time the lights came on there were no more than three hundred brave souls left in the stands, most of them die-hard British supporters who were more attuned to watching their sport in inhospitable weather. On top of the clubhouse, Dan Maskell and Gerald Williams shivered behind their microphones as they commentated for BBC Radio. 'No one had warned us about the freezing desert nights,' said Williams. 'But Buster's performance kept us going. He played some good matches for Britain but none better than this.'

Once Mottram had battled through a marathon third set to take it 10–8, he dominated the rest of the match to keep the Union Jack aloft. But it turned out to be a brave last stand in a remarkable campaign for Paul Hutchins's team.

David Lloyd's Davis Cup career still had a little way to run and the following year he and Cox teamed up successfully again to beat Manolo Orantes and José Higueras on grass at Eastbourne as Britain went through to the Zone final with a 4–1 victory over Spain. However, another tie against Italy meant a trip to the Foro Italico and despite another superb effort from Mottram, who shocked the Roman crowd by beating Panatta in straight sets, Britain could not manage another set in the entire tie and lost 4–1. Cox and the elder Lloyd tried all they knew to outwit Tonino Zugarelli and Corrado Barazzutti but went down 7–5, 10–8, 6–1.

The curtain came down on David's Davis Cup career at Bristol where he and his brother had the satisfaction of beating Dirzu and his old foe Nastase only to see John Feaver, controversially preferred to John Lloyd in the singles, lose the fifth rubber to Nastase to give Romania a 3–2 winning margin.

The older Lloyd looks back on his career with a modicum of satisfaction. 'There is no greater thrill or honour than playing for your country and I gave it my all,' he says. 'I wasn't a great player but I played to the full extent of my capabilities and maybe, on occasions, a bit above them. If you've done that, no one need call themselves a failure, no matter at what level you play the game.'

Chapter 4

Canada

Long before he established himself as a Davis Cup regular, David Lloyd had been trying to survive on a tour that was barely professional. Just a few years after Open Tennis had been sanctioned in 1968, most of the world's tournaments were still struggling to come to terms with the idea that tennis players could be paid legitimately as opposed to receiving unmarked envelopes under the table. Players like Rod Laver, Ken Rosewall and Arthur Ashe were already surpassing the seemingly huge sum of $100,000 a year in prize money on the WCT circuit but the money for the also-rans was minuscule and one needed wit and perseverence to survive. Lloyd, of course, was not lacking in either department, which was why he was able to finance trips to Africa by taking a suitcase full of dresses that had been earmarked for export at his father's office in the City and knock on some very unfamiliar doors in places like Nairobi, Lusaka and Bulawayo. He was seventeen at the time, but the art of turning a piece of cloth into a couple of bob was not new to him. As we have heard, John had watched him double the size of his pocket money at a much younger age, and if it worked at school in Essex why not in Nairobi?

That was the way David looked at it, anyway, and there were soon enough satisfied customers wearing smart new dresses to ensure that Lloyd was able to pay his hotel bill at the next tournament. He had a few contacts, of course; names given to him by his father. And there was also Abe Segal, the larger than life character immortalised in Gordon Forbes's classic tome *A Handful of Summers*, who was already active in the clothing business as his long-time doubles partnership with Forbes on court wound down.

'Abie helped me get the stuff into a couple of big stores in South

57

Africa,' says Lloyd. 'But a lot of the time it was just a question of knocking on doors and walking into shops. There wasn't much money in it, although it just about paid for the trip which was useful. But the real benefit was what it taught me about business and how you have to watch your backside. It taught me a lot about how some people offer you a fair bargain and how others try to con you if not actually rob you blind. It opened my eyes to a lot of things.'

He was wide-eyed, too, at the sights and sounds of that vast continent and enjoyed the experience — up to a point. The point came whenever he had to step onto another aeroplane. Strangely, for a young man who enjoyed fast cars, Lloyd hated flying, possibly for the reason so many people are uneasy in aircraft, because they are not in control. But, for anyone nervous about the whole business of being propelled into the air in a metal tube with wings attached, Africa in the Seventies was not the best place to test that nerve. The old DC3's and DC6's may have been the cargo workhorses of the air in World War II, but the problem was that many airlines were still flying the very same planes that had once been the pride of the US Air Force or had made the runs into Berlin during the airlift. There was a sticky tape and rubber band feel about them that often left you wondering where draught was coming from when you went to the lavatory. And on take off, with the cabin over-stuffed with crates, cartons and a few live chickens, it was difficult not to think of the American comedian Shelly Berman's great monologue on the joys of flying: 'And it rolls and it rolls and it rolls, doesn't it? And you think, to hell with science, tonight it's not going to make it. Tonight we're doomed . . .'

Lloyd thought about that sort of stuff too much, and suddenly he could take no more. A little while later, John Barrett arranged for him to play the South African Sugar Circuit as it was known in those days and his ticket was on Sabena with a stop in Brussels.

'And that was as far as I got,' says David. 'I got off the plane in Brussels and couldn't get back on. I just couldn't. I phoned JB in London and said, "Listen, I'm sorry, but I can't get back on another plane." So I ended up walking around Brussels all night thinking what a bloody idiot I was. I mean, JB had really put himself out to get me a place on the Sugar Circuit, which was a pretty high standard in those days, and it would have been a leg up for me. But there was no way. I didn't fly for another four years.'

But that, of course, did not prevent him playing the circuit, at least in Europe. Piling pals and odd pieces of merchandise in the back of the car (he discovered there was a good market for gut in Germany at the time), Lloyd would set off to play all the usual European events in places like Hamburg, Baden-Baden, Gstaad and Kitzbühel. He loved cars; loved driving them around the tortuous European roads, greeting every twist in a mountain pass as another challenge. Often he would have John Clifton, one of the Barrett Boys, with him in his sporty little Fiat 850 as they followed the young Australian Davis Cup player John Alexander who was also a car freak and had just bought himself a Rover 2000. It was difficult to know which was operating on higher octane fuel, the Fiat or David. Pure adrenalin and the zestful energy of youth enabled him to drive for hours before stepping out from behind the wheel and going straight on court. Lunch and sleep came later. Most of it was fun but once, in Kitzbühel, Lloyd let his temper get the better of him. Ironically, he was playing Alexander's great mate and doubles partner Phil Dent who had been JA's co-driver as they roared through the Alps.

'I was playing pretty well at the time and fancied my chances of winning that day,' Lloyd remembers. 'It was on the old Centre Court at Kitzbühel, the one with those big wooden stands, and at some stage of the match Phil did something cunning that got me annoyed; something that I felt was stretching the rules a bit. And so I go charging up to the net and have this big argument, shouting and screaming and I think I walked off in the end. Then I got straight in the car and drove all the way to North Berwick in Scotland — non-stop. Well, I think I got out of the car at Harwich and had a gallon of black coffee, but otherwise I drove without a break. God knows how many miles that is, but if you have a look at a map it's a fair distance. But that's where the next tournament was so off I went!'

So fear of flying did not restrict Lloyd's tournament schedule as much as it might have done, but he obviously needed to get over it somehow and help came from quite close to home. Francis Wallis had been one of the senior members of the Essex county team when David first started playing at that level, and several years later they were playing an International Club match together for Great Britain against France in Paris. By then Wallis had started the Wallis supermarket chain and was wealthy enough to have his own plane. When Lloyd told him about his flying problem, Wallis offered to take him up for a ride.

'He said I could sit in the co-pilot's seat and he'd show me how things worked. That helped a hell of a lot, actually. Somehow it just made it easier to accept. The tragedy of the story was that he was killed a few years later taking off in bad weather after an International Club match in the South of France. His doubles partner, Leslie Cater, and another Connaught member who was also a good player, Jock Kaley, were also killed. It was a real shocker. But I owe Francis a great deal. He was a lovely man and I'm pleased that there are a couple of courts at the Connaught Club which were donated from his trust fund. It would be a bit difficult today if I still had to drive everywhere!'

David kept playing on the Grand Prix circuit throughout the Seventies, sponsored at various times by Commercial Union, Colgate and Volvo. But although the sponsorship money was starting to create millionaires like Bjorn Borg, Guillermo Vilas and Jimmy Connors at the top of the tree, the pickings were slim down at Lloyd's end of the computer ranking and he had realised long before that he would need to find other ways of securing the future for himself and his family.

So he took himself off to Goirle in Holland and signed up with the Pellikaan Club in the Dutch league — a lucrative and highly competitive inter-club programme of a type that is even bigger in Germany. It was just the sort of format that suited David's style and skills, and after joining the club in 1975, he finally helped them break the monopoly that the Amsterdam club, Popeye, had exercised on the competition for years when Pellikaan won the title in 1979. Fred Hemmes, a top Dutch player of the period, was club captain and managed to remain relatively calm when his top foreign star disappeared one day, the week of an important match, to fly to Florida.

'I had to,' Lloyd laughs. 'John was getting married to Chrissie and I was best man. So I dashed over to London, flew to Miami and was back in time for the match that Sunday. But it all worked out great because we won the title.'

The Pellikaan club was owned by a wealthy builder called Hank Pellikaan who had built it, basically, to have somewhere for his son and himself to play tennis. He has three clubs now and has remained close to Lloyd, so much so that two of the DL Leisure Centres, Chigwell and Birmingham, have been built by Pellikaan. But back then, in between hurling himself about the court, Lloyd took good stock of his surroundings and, if one can trace the exact time and place where the first seed was planted, it must have been here, in this small Dutch town just across the strip of water that is part English Channel, part North Sea, not so very far from David's Essex home, but a world away in concept of what a comfortable and attractive sporting environment was all about. Gazing up from time to time as he sat on the bench cheering on his team mates, Lloyd took note of the beautiful wood fittings that secured the roof.

'And the nicely carpeted courts and well-run restaurant and bar — just the whole atmosphere of those clubs made me think, How come we don't have ANYTHING like this at home when they have scores of them over here?'

It was a question he couldn't answer and it bugged him.

He had already been looking farther afield to fill in the time when he was not actually playing on the tour and, in 1974, he started to get a feel about what was on offer in North America when he joined the fledgling World Team Tennis League which was Billie Jean King's baby — a truncated form of the game that featured one-set matches and multi-coloured courts with everyone encouraged to hoop and holler, as the Americans might say. It all seemed a very long way from Wimbledon, but it was highly competitive and a lot of fun. Lloyd joined a team called the Minnesota Buckskins in Minneapolis where his team mates were Britain's very own Wimbledon champion, Ann Jones, and a couple of Aussies, Wendy Turnbull and Owen Davidson. A lot of the matches were played in private clubs, and Lloyd was overwhelmed by the grandeur and wealth of these places. Wanting more, inquisitive and determined to learn everything he could about how a game he had played all his life was housed and presented in North America, Lloyd started looking around for other opportunities and eventually ended up applying for a job at the Wingfield Racket Club in Toronto. He had to fudge his credentials a bit because he went after the post of Director of Tennis.

'I said I had run coaching programmes and things which was just about true,' he says. 'But life is all about luck and timing. Frankly, I think I got the job because they liked my accent — reminded a few of them of the old country — and then, after I had been there no more than about a month, the owner got rid of the General Manager and I took his place. There I was running the whole club. It was an unbelievable experience and I learned so many things that were to come in useful later.'

Lloyd found he enjoyed running a club. He enjoyed the diversity of it and he enjoyed fixing things — everything from the shower that ran cold to the boiler that wouldn't boil. The members were a good bunch, too, 90 per cent Jewish and David loved their sense of humour and the business acumen they displayed. He could relate to that. It led, a little later, to a brief but highly enjoyable coaching visit to Tel Aviv where the South African-born Ian Froman was in the process of building up Israeli tennis to the point where he is now tournament director of the popular Eisenberg Israel Tennis Open, a world series event on the ATP Tour.

But much as Lloyd would have liked to spend more time there, something was calling him home. He had left Toronto because it had just been a six-month job while he was off the circuit but, quite apart from teaching him a good deal about how to run a tennis club, he found it helped his game when he returned to the tour. To some extent the pressure was off. He had proved to himself that he had something to turn to when it was time to stop. Few people who have never tried to earn a living from professional sport can quite comprehend the anxiety factor that sits on a competitor's shoulder every step of the way out to the middle at Lord's, or round the final bend of the 400 metres at Crystal Palace, or standing there waiting to receive at match point at Wimbledon or even Barcelona, Hamburg or Tel Aviv. It may be a jolly nice game to the spectators in the stands, but finishing first or fifth or missing that match point by an inch instead of making it can ultimately decide where you are able to send your son to school. This is heavy baggage to carry into the competitive arena and, with young Scotty a factor in his life following his marriage to Veronica, it weighed on David's mind.

'It was always a worry in those days,' he admits. 'Obviously a lot more players make a lot more money now, but the question of What do I do when I stop? was always hanging over you then and I am sure it affected my game. It was a constant worry and too often I found myself wondering if I was making enough to justify the whole strange lifestyle. Once I satisfied myself that I could probably make a decent living for the family doing something else, my tennis improved a bit.'

And in those closing years of the Seventies, while he watched his younger brother marry the Wimbledon champion and become a familiar face in the world's glossy magazines, David allowed the germ of an idea at the back of his mind to grow and grow.

'I'd taken a close look at the operation in Toronto and I knew it had to work in Britain. We had nothing like it. The weather wasn't as cold but it was just as wet and people had nowhere decent to play. The more I thought about it, the more I became convinced that it was a feasible idea. John Barrett agreed with me but there were precious few others. I can't tell how many people at the Queen's Club, people I regarded as friends to varying degrees, told me I was out of my mind. Some just laughed outright; others told me not to waste my money. But, above all, it was the apathy that got to me most. It permeated the whole place, not just Queen's, which was falling to bits, but right next door at the LTA where everyone sat around waiting for something to happen; waiting for another Rod Laver to drop from the sky. Life isn't like that. You've got to make things happen. Not at some distant point in time but NOW. I just couldn't hang around for people to get their minds in gear and understand what I was on about. There wasn't time. I was impatient to achieve something; make a contribution; fill a void which was a great yawning gap in British tennis as far as I could see. But an awful lot of doors were closed in my face before I could get any real support.'

Chapter 5

Setting Up

With the experience of Holland, Canada and Israel behind him, David Lloyd returned to Britain in 1978 at a pivotal moment in his career. The playing of the game he loved was winding down and he knew it was the moment to make a move.

'I wasn't going to hang around and make the same mistake I had seen so many players make — wait three or four years after they had virtually stopped playing. By that time nobody knows them, they're on the way down and maybe they don't have the opportunity to put their own money into a business venture. I said to myself, "I'm not going to make that mistake", so I started to make use of the contacts I had and, actually, it was Keith Wooldridge, one of the Barrett Boys, who came up with the best suggestion. He knew this guy who was a developer, John Dunningham, who had a lovely place in Cookham Dean. He likes tennis and plays a bit but is a mad keen golfer, a member at Wentworth, and now plays quite a bit with some other tennis friends of mine, Harry and Carole Matheson. Anyway, we went down there to talk to him and he said that he couldn't really help us himself but he knew a chap called Bob Reynolds who was Chief Planning Officer for Hounslow Council. This was one of the areas I had been thinking of because the M4 was the busiest road in Britain at the time and the M25 was just being thought about. And then there was the airport. So, as everybody had been telling me "location, location, location", I thought, this has to be the right place. We'd had a demographic study done and it estimated that there would be 2.6 million people within half an hour of the site. So I thought, "Geez, we only need 3,000, that's not a lot of people."

'So I went to see Bob Reynolds and he said that a modern,

multi-facility tennis club was something they would really like in the Borough and suddenly I had a site — a site and £100,000 of my own money which I'd saved through mortgaging the house, and a dream. Soon, I also had a plan. It was drawn up by an architect, Trevor Freeman, who is still working with me here at the Arena. He did it on the basis of a no-job, no-fee thing. Then we had a model made which cost a couple of thousand quid, but at least we had something to show to people.

'I did a lot of the feasibility studies sitting in John Barrett's living room at his house near Kingston. I used to stay with him a lot when I was a Barrett Boy, so it was like home from home to me and JB was encouraging me all the way. I used to pore over all these figures and make assumptions like "if a thousand members paid £500 each, etc", and eventually we put together a business plan and a cash flow projection and all the things you have to do and we reckoned we needed to raise £1.2 million, which was even more money in those days. But we were cautious with those figures. Too many people get carried away and try to look on the optimistic side. As far as forecasting is concerned you have to be pessimistic. You can't manipulate figures — they are what they are. We did ours based on a 70 per cent occupancy at what we reckoned was a low membership fee. We could have survived on that. But in fact when we opened we got 100 per cent, so immediately we were in business.'

David Lloyd and Charles Haswell make an unlikely pair — Lloyd, the pugnacious little pigeon-toed street fighter and Haswell, tall and shy, languid in appearance and personality. Lloyd, the self-made man — although only half self-made at the time they hooked up — and Haswell, the rich man's son with his public school accent who, like so many of us, would have loved to be a great player but whose ability tethered him to the middle echelons of the Queen's Club membership.

But it was, of course, this love of the game that brought them into contact. Haswell's father had made his millions as an engineer of international repute. The tunnel connecting Kowloon with Hong Kong Island stands as his finest memorial, and before his death he was acting as a consultant on the Channel Tunnel, making three visits to the site when construction began. It was the success of the

Hong Kong contract, which included work on the much praised mass transit system, which ensured the financial security of the Haswell family, and by the time that was built young Charles had reaped some of the dividends. Thankfully, for everyone now enjoying the facilities of David Lloyd Leisure, Charles was not one of those young men who rush out and spend Daddy's money on fast Ferraris and beautiful blondes. As it turned out it was David who would end up with the Ferrari and Charles the blonde, but that was down the road after a lot of hard work had been accomplished. Being a keen tennis player and an equally keen observer of the desultory state of the game in Britain, Haswell thought he might be able to make a contribution to its improvement. So he wrote to the LTA and subsequently met briefly with the then chairman, Geoff Brown.

'I told him I had about £100,000 to invest in some project that might help British tennis, and at the beginning of the Eighties that was not a small sum of money,' said Haswell. 'He sounded interested and promised he would write to me.'

Incredibly — although, given their track record at the time, perhaps not so incredibly — the LTA never replied. This, after all, was the organisation that had nearly fainted when Bob Brett, already established as one of the world's leading coaches, had suggested a salary of $75,000 to take charge of British tennis. That was in the late Eighties and was the going price at the time. A few years later Ion Tiriac, with his proven track record of having taken Guillermo Vilas to the top of the game and nurtured Boris Becker's phenomenal rise, met with LTA officials at the Monte Carlo Open. His offer was typically challenging. Tiriac wanted $250,000 with the proviso that it would be returned in its entirety if he had failed to produce a top 50 British player within three years. It was a challenge the LTA failed to take up.

Brett and Tiriac did not, of course, hang about pleading on the LTA's doorstep at Baron's Court. They took their expertise elsewhere and that was Britain's loss. Fortunately Haswell was as determined as he was forgiving, because the kind of behaviour meted out to this well-meaning, would-be benefactor, would have been enough to crush any feelings of goodwill someone might have harboured towards the game. Haswell, however, was not going to allow the rebuff of silence to deter him. Shortly afterwards he was playing golf with Roger Becker and Tommy Baldwin, the footballer who was on Chelsea's books at the time, and Roger mentioned that David Lloyd was trying to raise funds to build a tennis club. At the time, Lloyd thought he might have a Dutch investor on board but the man* shortly afterwards withdrew and Haswell contacted him.

'I told David I had £125,000 to invest and with his £100,000 that would be enough to enable us to approach an investment banker to try and raise the rest,' Haswell recalls.

But first, Haswell wanted to run the proposal past an accountant friend of his, Victor Clements, who worked at a firm which was then called Rowland Nevill, later to become Moores Rowland. Lloyd, knowing there was no way round this procedure, reluctantly agreed. 'I took my nice little plans and feasibility studies along to Charles's accountant and held my breath,' says Lloyd. 'Normally you have no chance — and I mean NO chance — of convincing an accountant. Usually they're looking at all the negatives and that, in my opinion, is the trouble with British business — negatives, negatives. But to my surprise this guy liked it and recommended that Charles put some money in.'

In the meantime, Haswell was searching for a financial institution willing to come up with a bit of funding. He approached his own bank, the Royal Bank of Scotland, and was turned down not once but twice. Mistake, big mistake. Or as Julia Roberts said so memorably to the shop assistant in *Pretty Woman*, 'Huge'. Unhappily for

---

*The man was Gies Van de Pluim who ran a tournament in Holland and had a daughter, Babette, who wanted to be a tennis player. She was actually being coached by Roger Becker and staying at the Lloyds' house near Esher at the time while Lloyd was involved in business with her father. 'My job was to persuade editors of magazines to give a page of advertising for the Dutch prints he was trying to sell in return for free framed prints as prizes for their readers. It was fun for a while but the quality of the frames wasn't good enough so I called it off. Ultimately Van de Pluim decided not to invest in the club. Babette went on to be a doctor in sports medicine; I still see her occasionally.'

the Bank's executives there is rather a splendid reminder of just how much money they could have made out of the deal every time they drive to Glasgow Airport. Unless you deliberately avert your eyes, there is little chance of avoiding the sign adorning the second largest club of its kind in Britain — David Lloyd Leisure Centre.

Clements finally led them to Midland Montague Ventures and an introduction to Ernie Cole, who was head of Midland Montague, and Ian Taylor, from the bank's Venture Capital arm, who was to become so involved with the scheme that, several years later when he retired, he went to work for Lloyd as his Managing Director. It was no coincidence that Taylor was a keen tennis player and a member of the Hurlingham Club where courts are in plentiful supply. It followed the first rule in the search for sponsorship or financial funding in sports management — find the executive who is in love with the sport you are peddling. Golf's success is based almost entirely on this tenet. Better still in this instance, Taylor's interest was even more specific than just liking the game of tennis. He had felt strongly for some years that the game in Britain desperately needed indoor facilities and had been actively searching for someone to front the kind of operation Lloyd had in mind.

'In the course of that search, I had spoken to one or two names who were a lot bigger than David's,' said Taylor. 'But I hadn't been sufficiently impressed to follow up. David was completely different. First of all he was prepared to do it all himself. He was not only totally involved with his idea but he was bright and numerically adept. Brilliant with figures. To our eyes in the City, he was far from being a sophisticated businessman at that stage but he learned and learned very fast.'

Taylor remembers his first meeting with David being held at Samuel Montague's offices in the City. Samuel Montague was the sister company of Midland Montague Ventures who would normally take care of any equity investment. It was a preliminary talk followed by a couple more in which John Barrett joined. Taylor knew that Lloyd had already been approached by Barratt the builders who were interested in a different kind of deal. They were looking for a building opportunity and offered to come in for 50 per cent of the stake — a deal that would mean Lloyd would not fully own or be free to develop his dream. 'In fact I would have lost control totally in a matter of months because they would have put more money in and I would not have been able to match it,' says Lloyd.

'Absolutely right,' agrees Taylor. 'A year down the road, they would have said, "Oh, we need to inject a bit more cash into this operation — here's our million, where's yours?" And in no time at all they would have had control.'

Originally, Lloyd had been keen on the Barratt offer because it would at least get the club built when no one else at that stage seemed interested in putting in any money at all.

'In fact I was getting pretty frustrated by then,' he admits. 'I had been to so many people; begging at times, and it had all taken so long that I desperately wanted to get the damned thing built. I knew it wasn't an ideal deal but it was a deal and I was anxious to get on with it.'

So Lloyd, to Taylor's surprise, came to a verbal agreement with Barratt. 'I read about it in the *Evening Standard* on my way home one day,' Taylor recalls. 'I was pretty upset because I thought I was in the middle of active negotiations with David. But it turned out to be something of an exaggeration and, after a bit of cunning planning, I got the thing to swing back our way.'

It may not have been as exaggerated as Taylor thinks. Lloyd had got as far as setting up a press conference for the week after Wimbledon 1981 to be held at the Kensington Hilton in Holland Park, a well-known tennis location because the hotel had been used for many years by the players competing at the old Benson & Hedges at Wembley. Lloyd had made his mind up and, especially in those days, the Thatcherite dogma was his by-word. Under almost all circumstances, he was not for turning. And had it not been for a chance meeting with Haswell, Lloyd would have driven straight into Barratt's clutches and, unable to control his own destiny, a very uncertain future.

But fate, as so often happens when something is obviously supposed to take root, took a hand. On the final Saturday evening Haswell happened to dine at an Italian restaurant near the area now known as Chelsea Harbour and ran into a large party celebrating the victory of one Mrs J. M. Lloyd, better known as Chris Evert, over Hana Mandlikova earlier that day. After two losing appearances in the final, it was Chrissie's first Wimbledon triumph since her marriage to John so there was much to celebrate. However that did not prevent Charles and David getting into a fearful argument on the pavement as they left the restaurant. Haswell remembers it well.

'It was the only time in a relationship that has now lasted over fifteen years that David and I have had a real, raging argument,' he says. 'He was set on the Barratt deal and was about to turn his back on Midland Montague Ventures after just a couple of preliminary meetings despite the fact that, in my opinion, they had a more interesting offer to make. I pleaded with him just to meet with them again before he actually signed the Barratt deal and eventually lost my temper. I couldn't believe he wouldn't at least meet with them to hear what they had to say. "How can you lose?" I asked him. "Just see them!" '

They must have made a strange pair, Haswell towering over his feisty little partner, raising his voice in a manner that would have shocked anyone who knew him at the time. Charles was not noted for his forceful opinions in those days. Sweet and meek are descriptions one would have applied to his personality, but we were underestimating him. In his quiet, diffident sort of way, he could be as stubborn as the man who was busy re-defining the word! Yet, if he couldn't quite initiate a U-turn, he did manage to get Lloyd to pull over before he charged any farther down the Barratt motorway.

David laughs at the memory now. 'Yeah, Charles is right about that. He did get pretty insistent about it and finally I thought, what the hell, we might as well talk to them one more time. So we met with the people from Midland Montague. It was at the All England Club, actually, and we went upstairs to the old players' cafeteria as it existed then and listened to their offer.'

It was 1981, the year John McEnroe won his first Wimbledon, gaining revenge over Bjorn Borg for the famous tie-break classic that he had lost to the Swede the previous year. On the outside courts that year one could have glimpsed Peter McNamara winning a couple of tie-breaks against the flute-playing Californian hippie Jeff Borowiak, and Vijay Amritraj using his classic serve to quell the unfulfilled talent of the Australian Paul Kronk. These men hit the ball hard and the thwack of ball on gut would have echoed up into the All England Club's first-floor restaurant. Lloyd was not in his tennis clothes when he met the men in suits from the City but he might as well have been. Apart from a few minor business ventures, he had done nothing in his whole life except travel the world and play tennis. Now he was pitching himself into big-time negotiating with experts who had spent even more hours in board rooms than he had on a tennis court. But he wasn't scared. Nervous perhaps, but not scared. He knew what he wanted and he had the security of knowing that he had another deal to fall back on. So he listened and was soon liking what he heard.

'Basically, they were prepared to put up the same amount of money as Barratt but in a different way. Most venture capitalists will not take more than 30 per cent of normal equity. They don't want more because it would mean they would be in control and most merchant banks don't actually want to be in control. They are basically an investor looking for a very high rate of return. Venture capitalists are looking to make about 40 per cent return on their money. They take more risk. They take a lot of losses as a result but when they hit they usually hit big.

'So we are sitting up there in the lounge at Wimbledon with play going on on all the outside courts and Ian Taylor says to me, "We'll put in for 30 per cent but we'll also put in preference shares." They are non-voting shares, carrying a dividend of 10 per cent, and there-fore you can build up this amount of money and then you can get a bank loan. I thought that sounded pretty good but I wanted some-thing else. So I said, "That's fine but I want 'A' and 'B' shares." 'A' shares are voting shares and I wanted to make sure that whatever happened with this deal, I would retain some sort of control. I want-ed some flesh and blood in there, not just a business deal on paper.

'I saw instantly that this was going to be a much better deal than the one Barratt were offering but I needed time to go away and think about it. My head was spinning with all this share business. After all, I was only a tennis player at the time! But it didn't take me long to realise that we couldn't refuse. I felt badly about Barratt and they were mad as hell when I told them that I was cancelling the press conference and that our deal was off.'

A few days later the tennis player was wearing his best suit and tie as he and Haswell arrived at the offices of Midland Montague Ventures in Poultry Lane near the Mansion House. There was no sound of tennis balls being hit on green lawns outside the window this time. Just the roar of red buses and London traffic. This was the City — the Wimbledon of the financial world — and David Lloyd was playing for higher stakes than he had ever done on a tennis court. He was nervous but he was used to that. You are always nervous before a big match. As any tennis player will tell you, there is a huge difference between being nervous and choking.

To choke — as in becoming paralysed with fear — is the worst humiliation a player can suffer. Some players learn how to handle it, others never do and consequently totally fail to fulfil their true potential. Rod Laver, a neighbour of Dennis and Doris Lloyd when the couple winter at John's place at Rancho Mirage, California, explains it from the perspective of a champion.

'Everybody gets nervous, that's natural,' says Laver, still the only man to have done the Grand Slam (winning all four major championships in one year) in the Open era. 'The question is: How do you handle it? If you panic about the very fact of being nervous, then you're choking and you fall apart. You're standing there at match point on the Centre Court at Wimbledon and everything starts to tense up and you've just got to say to yourself, Yeah, that's OK. Bit nervous now but I'll just give this next one a bit of a nudge. Just accept the fact you're nervous, don't try and fight it.'

Laver was famous for giving a tennis ball a bit of a nudge with a freckled left arm that seemed to have been borrowed from Popeye. David Lloyd, although powerfully built, had no such physical weapon but his instincts were not too dissimilar to Laver's. When crunch time arrived, he went for it. But, again like Laver, it was not a blind swing. When the man they called the Rockhampton Rocket hit a tennis ball, he knew exactly where he wanted it to go, even if, in his youth, he would sometimes miss by yards. When Lloyd hung tough around a bargaining table the thump he gave it was usually tempered by a tactical plan although he, too, could be guilty of allowing that temper to blur the precision of his thinking.

Midland Montague were to discover this very quickly. Lloyd wanted his 'A' shares and he wanted control. That was his goal and he never let his eye wander from the ball, not even when unfamiliar business procedure kept cropping up seemingly to complicate what, to his still simplistic business mind, was supposed to be a straight-forward deal. There he was, poised with pen in hand, as impatient as if it were a racket and he was waiting to receive serve, and Ernie Cole, the head of Midland Montague Ventures, was trying to explain that the money would come from two different sources, Midland Montague and Capulet.

'Who the hell is Capulet?' asked Lloyd, whose school curriculum had not included *Romeo and Juliet*.

'It's one of our shell companies at the investment end of the business,' Cole explained, revealing, perhaps, that someone in the banking world had a romantic sense of humour. As the houses of Montague and Capulet spend most of Shakespeare's play insulting each other, the thought of putting them to bed together in the same financial deal was obviously irresistible. Initially the two companies each put up 50 per cent of the money but that was not the only 50:50 deal in the offing. For internal reasons, Montague wanted the contract signed on a 50:50 basis with the share holdings evenly held between the bank and Lloyd. But that was done in the full knowledge of what Lloyd's next move would be.

'We signed and almost before the ink was dry I bought one of my brother's shares. That left John with 9,999 'B' shares but the one he sold to me tipped the balance and, with my 100,000 'A' shares, I had control.'

So the whole thing went smoothly? Well, not quite. Incredibly, Lloyd had nearly walked away from the whole thing because of the price of a car!

'I was all ready to sign and we came to my personal contracts. I said I wanted a company car and, as far as I was concerned, it had to be an Audi Quattro. Great car! It was the first four-wheel drive and I had set my heart on it. I've always been crazy about cars and this was my dream machine. But when we came to this item Hugh de Corvanne said the limit was £11,000 on a car and the Audi cost £15,000 at the time. We were talking about a £4,000 difference on a deal worth over a million quid, but we were both as stubborn as each other and neither of us would back down. I was prepared to walk away from it — I really was. It was the principle of the thing.'

Faced with match point, Lloyd didn't choke. What he did, in fact, was both bloody-minded and brilliant — typical David. He phoned up Audi and persuaded them to give him a sponsor's car with 1,000 miles on the clock for £11,000. 'So I got the car I wanted and they never knew the difference. I never told Hugh.'

Signing the deal provided a major launching pad for David Lloyd's dream, but there were still almost as many technical and bureaucratic obstacles to overcome as NASA faces before firing another rocket into space. Perhaps you didn't need to be a rocket scientist to solve them, but more ingenuity, patience and bloody-minded determination were needed than most rookie entrepreneurs would have been capable of mustering at such an early stage of their careers.

'Patience, of course, was never my strong point, but I did learn to battle on and try to find a way round problems rather than always charging in feet first,' says Lloyd. 'I wasn't always successful, of course. I blew my top on occasions and I learned the hard way that explosions don't always bring the best results. But it was so exasperating to run into people who just didn't grasp what you were on about or just refused to admit that you might have a good idea.'

And then there was the Council, aided and abetted, in Lloyd's eyes at least, by the lawyers. In all his enthusiasm and naivety, Lloyd had thought everything was going to be fine once he had secured the money and found the parcel of land just down the road from the Western Markets International warehouses at Heston. But there are awkward things like sewerage and electricity to be worked out, and suddenly a developer can find himself entangled in a bureaucratic bog almost as foul-smelling as the stuff he is trying to dispose of.

'You wouldn't believe the clauses and sub-clauses and the way the lawyers cover every possible eventuality, no matter how unlikely, on behalf of their client — and all for sums of money that still, to this day, I find quite incredible. If Ian Taylor hadn't been such a clever and flexible banker I don't know what we would have done.'

Taylor kept probing away to find solutions to the kind of Catch 22 problems that send rational men almost mad with frustration. The lease said that the disposal pipe for the foul sewage was on a line to be agreed by the Council. But the lawyers, dotting every 'i' and crossing every 't', said that 'to be agreed' can mean never because you haven't actually agreed. Therefore, in all their legal wisdom, they recommended to Midland Montague that they refuse to sign the contract. There are some bankers in this world who would have taken fright at that and walked away. But Taylor, who had heard all this legalese before, called everybody's bluff and told David that he would work with him to find a solution. So they got out the plans and found a place for the sewer on a field adjacent to the club site and marked out a route to it across another field owned by a private individual, thus allowing them to bypass Council property.

'It wasn't very far but it wasn't direct either and it would have cost us about £100,000 extra to get it done,' says Lloyd. 'Eventually we got it worked out with the Council because they saw how stupid the whole situation was becoming. But I feel that a lot of it could have been avoided if the lawyers had not dwelt on the worst case scenario as they always seem to.'

But there was more to come. Having solved the sewerage, there was the gas. The problem with the gas was tied in with the hill that Lloyd didn't want but which the Council made him build. Not a terribly large hill, but large enough so that it would hide the outline of the building from certain viewpoints along the road. Lloyd actually wanted to use the space for a carpark but the council said no, he would have to build this little hill which is still there to this day. The only hills in Heston tend to be man-made.

'So we built this bloody hill and then went to see about the gas. Well, just in case you didn't know, there is a law about gas — one relating to the distance from which the gas company will supply it. The distance is 25 metres, which would have been fine if the hill hadn't pushed the clubhouse farther away from the road. But it had. So we couldn't get any gas. This time the solution was to build a half-way house. Just a little house which is still there now and which serves no purpose other than to meet the legality of not having British Gas serve us at a distance of more than 25 metres. It's 25 metres to the house and another 23 metres on to the club-house. Don't ask me how much that cost us but I'm sure somebody enjoyed the whole situation.'

There were moments when Lloyd was close to despair — nights when he went home to Veronica and asked her if she thought he really was mad and should they pack it in. But it was never a serious question and Veronica knew it. There may have been terriers who have clasped a bone between their teeth harder than David Lloyd, but it is unlikely. He would growl and scratch and wag his tail until such time as others would let him have his bone, and by then there was no doubt as to how deep his teeth marks would be. But it would be his bone, fashioned in his image, and no one was going to take it from him.

He had done his homework. The architects' plans had been pored over and the potential cash flow figures checked and re-checked. To some extent he was surmising; taking educated guesses because nothing quite like the club he was intending to build existed in Britain at the time. The old private clubs operated on a different financial structure, and the leisure centres that did exist were not as complex or diverse. But, in his mind's eye, he knew exactly what he wanted to create. It was the look of the indoor tennis halls that gave Heston its unique feel and has become a feature of all his clubs since. It was the wood; the light, laminated wood beams that brightened up the tennis halls and gave them a warmer, more welcoming feel than any ever seen in Britain before. Again it was David's Dutch connection that gave him the idea. The clubs he had worked at in Holland all had wooden beams acting as roof supports, and everyone he spoke to there and in Germany had told him that wood was safer than metal.

'Metal bends when it gets hot,' Lloyd explains. 'Wood just chars but doesn't bend. In the case of a fire, the buckling metal causes the roof to collapse in minutes, whereas these beams are so thick that they burn through very slowly. It took us a bit of time to persuade the local Council engineers, who are a cautious lot, that this was true. Charles Haswell's father's firm was a big help with this because they were top engineers and knew that we were right.'

Lloyd was fascinated by the process and, typically, got so involved with it that he formed a company called David Lloyd Sports Centres with a view to manufacturing the beams and selling them to other sports centres. Two other firms, Mowlands and Nemaho, came in with him on a one-third each basis, but the idea never really got off the ground, partly because prospective buyers saw Lloyd as a competitor and wouldn't deal with him. 'People are so suspicious of each other, it's incredible,' he says. 'I'm not afraid of anyone pinching my ideas. I just want to do some business.' But nobody would, so the company lies dormant while more and more beams are made for more and more David Lloyd Leisure Centres.

'The actual process is interesting because they make these beams with planks of untreated, horrible-looking soft wood. They are about four inches deep by about eight feet, and they shave them off and then actually glue them together. Then they lay them out on this gigantic floor to make sure they actually hold the fit and the shape. They can do any size and any shape because wood like that is more flexible than metal and will bend into any shape you want. The colour is almost white to start with but then begins to change to a darker shade after a few weeks in the hall. It's not treated in any way. You see it used a lot in German churches and I think we've convinced a few people now that it is not only practical and safe but far nicer to look at than metal girders.'

With the building taking shape, it was time for Lloyd to get his team together. And it was inevitable that, with John Barrett's guidance, he would turn to the Slazenger chief, Buzzer Hadingham, as his choice for Chairman of the Board. Hadingham was not only a man of great charm and humour but, apart from knowing the commercial side of the game as well as anyone in Britain, he was also a member of the All England Club committee with all the clout and contacts that come with that rarefied position. Even allowing for the disappointment which surrounded Slazenger's ultimate refusal to invest directly in the club, Hadingham proved a popular and supportive Chairman until his elevation to a somewhat more exalted chairmanship at Wimbledon necessitated his departure.

It was no surprise when Lloyd then turned to his old Davis Cup captain Headley Baxter to fill Hadingham's chair. Baxter was one of the few people closely connected with the running of the game in Britain at that time to whom one instinctively turned for good advice and down-to-earth common sense. I was one of those who felt that, had he been given Basil Reay's old job at the LTA, British tennis would have benefitted enormously. But Baxter was one of those people who speak their mind and he didn't much care who liked it and who didn't. His words were frequently considered too potent a medicine for the more timid members of the LTA Committee of Management and so Headley, a stalwart of Middlesex tennis for many years, remained on the fringes of power. He and David Lloyd were inevitably drawn to each other and the fact that they were such good friends made the subsequent falling out all the more painful.

But there was no hint of the troubles that lay ahead as Lloyd busied himself with the final months of preparation for the realisation of his dream. Right up to the last minute, nothing could be taken for granted.

Insight I

Frustration

'Trying to get financial institutions to invest or to lend us money for the first club at Heston proved one of the most frustrating experiences of my life. I felt everything about the site and the concept was right but I couldn't get "the men in suits" — many of whom were younger than me so it was not a generation problem — to understand or appreciate what I was talking about. I might have been talking in another language for all the mutual understanding there was.

The most frustrating meeting of all actually occurred after I had raised the £1.6 million I needed to build Heston. Philip Wilkinson liked the concept so much that he wanted his investment bank, Nat West County, to put in some equity. So I went up to their offices in the City and was ushered into this room with all this beautiful wood panelling and portraits on the walls. I'm sitting there admiring all this and then this chap comes in with white gloves carrying a silver platter and pours me a cup of tea. Then all these directors file in and they're quite a young group which I thought was a good sign and I'm sipping my tea, full of expectation, and I explain that I want to open a tennis centre. I show them the plans and this chap across the table says, "Where's the nearest bus stop?" So I ask him if he plays golf and he said he did so then I say, "And how do you get there?" and sure enough he says by car. So I say, "Well, that's how you're going to get to my club." Then another guy said, "What's it worth as a warehouse?" and I said, "I'm not building a bloody warehouse, I'm building a tennis centre!" It was just the most negative meeting you could imagine and finally I picked up my stuff and left. It's the attitude *that gets to me. I just don't understand it. Nor do I get much satisfaction from the fact that if they had put in the kind of money Philip Wilkinson was suggesting, they would have watched £250,000 grow into fifty million in twelve years. To me it's just pure frustration.*

Chapter 6

Heston

The paint was still wet; some of the concrete barely dry. Tarpaulins covered an unbuilt bit at the back. But basically the David Lloyd Leisure Centre at Heston was open. And David Lloyd was in tears. Not just a moist little trickle, either. The man was in trouble. When he took the microphone to officially open his club and declare his dream reality, he got through a couple of sentences and had to stop. He was sobbing.

That simple incident revealed to all of us present just what this thing meant to David Lloyd. He put his reputation on the line and risked his financial future on a scheme that an untold number of people — intelligent, well-informed, well-meaning people — had described as madness. But his gut feeling told him he was right and his hell-or-high-water, this is going to fail over my dead body approach to life ensured that he would be more right than even his greatest supporters had dared imagine.

Cautious as ever with his figures, David and Ian Taylor had stuck with their 70 per cent capacity for membership as a break-even figure and, to their astonishment, found their figure hopelessly conservative. A day after the club opened, the membership closed. Full. 'The kind of cash flow we generated from day one enabled David to build a fourth tennis hall within the first year,' said Taylor. 'It was basically that kind of response from the public putting their money down in significant numbers that generated the success of the whole operation. If you have a large cash flow you can secure loans to expand and one thing literally builds on the other.'

It nearly didn't get built at all. A couple of weeks before the scheduled opening, Lloyd was being told by his builders that they wouldn't be finished for a month or more. 'They said there was no way we were going to make it on time and I said, "Oh yes there bloody well is", and we did which was lucky, really, because about a month before we're due to open Willment, the builders, go bankrupt. Luckily the actual workers stayed with us even though they were no longer getting paid. They were fantastic. Of course we had to have the readies out, coming up with a few twenty quid notes to keep their interest up, but basically they were with us and got caught up in it all. It would have been a bit embarrassing to have a club 85 per cent built, but we got lucky. You always need the luck. So much of it, so much of life, is about timing. We squeaked in.'

It was a close call, however. David and his most supportive cohorts were slaving away until the early hours of the very morning the club opened. John Barrett, Tony Lloyd and Donald Watt, the Scottish touring pro who would end up as Manager at Renfrew several years later, were all there, wrestling with green backdrop canvasses on the courts and trying to drill holes in concrete. But Heston has big thick pillars dividing the courts and Tony couldn't make any impression on them with his drill. Barrett seized it from him but found that it just bounced off. This was reinforced concrete and a power drill was needed. Eventually one was found and everyone trooped out at 2.30 a.m., brushing the dust off their track suits and wondering how this building site had been transformed into something resembling a tennis club in such a short space of time.

However, there were many people in Britain in the early Eighties who would have had trouble recognising it as such. Apart from the upmarket establishments like the Queen's Club, which was in a poor state of repair in any case, and Hurlingham which was really a country club with tennis courts, the average tennis club in England pre-David Lloyd consisted of a cluster of not very well maintained courts huddled around a wooden structure that served as a clubhouse. Tea and buns were the staple diet, and if the showers were hot it was a miracle. In many clubs there were no showers. The nail in the wall on which to hang your shirt might have been an exaggeration but the general concept of spartan, make-do facilities was uncomfortably close to the norm. It wasn't that people didn't want anything better, but they were not prepared to pay enough to get anything better. Subscriptions were ridiculously low and no one had the vision or the gumption to break out of the rut of barely acceptable mediocrity.

In the pre-Thatcher era, getting an Englishman to part with his shilling made his Scottish cousin look like a spendthrift. I remember Annual General Meetings of the LTA that all but broke down over the demand for an extra half crown on the membership dues. People would rage over such an outrageous demand and then go and put six half crowns in the slot machine at the local pub. David Lloyd's genius was in building something that looked like a million dollars in comparison with anything they had seen before while charging sums of money they could easily afford. It might have been ten times as much as they had ever dreamt of paying for a tennis club membership before, but they had never dreamt of having anything as functional, comfortable and entertaining on their doorstep.

The amenities, of course, went far beyond anything provided by the average tennis club. An indoor pool, a gym equipped with the latest fitness machine, a dance class studio for aerobics, a billiard table, a creche for the infant, a spacious bar with a sunken area to watch television on a huge screen and a restaurant serving good food. All this and twelve indoor tennis courts and another ten outside. For £275 a year plus court charges? No wonder they were lining up. Affordable quality at a level far above anything else available is an irresistible commodity and David Lloyd had provided it.

If experts in the business had suggested the whole concept was mad then Lloyd compounded their belief by opening up a club for 2,000 with a staff of fifteen. Everyone had to muck in. It was the only way it could possibly work. 'You'd come off court after a couple of hours teaching and immediately go behind the bar,' Donald Watt recalls. 'And you did it because David was doing it. David opened and shut the club, and to start with we were open sixteen hours a day. We couldn't afford a security guard and David never felt inclined to trust them anyway, so he slept in his car several nights outside the front door. After about nine months he came up with the idea of giving members keys and keeping the club open twenty-four hours a day. It was brilliant. It solved the dead of night security problem and brought in more money because, believe it or not, there was quite heavy usuage in the early hours. With Heathrow so close, a lot of our members worked strange hours and fancied a game at two in the morning! But working for David was not easy in those early days. He had put everything he owned on the line so it was understandable that he drove everyone very hard. But he was brutal at times. However, if you were prepared to stick with it, everything turned out to be worthwhile.'

Many people were not prepared to stick with it and some never got the chance. Like the duty manager whom David discovered one evening with his feet up on the desk. 'You're out!' said David, incensed. 'Go on! Out that door!' Fired on the spot. And there were plenty of others, too. Staff turnover at Heston in the first couple of years was pretty brisk because it was difficult to find people who shared Lloyd's level of commitment. And of those who did have the commitment, several couldn't handle the man's abrasive personality. Because he knew every nook and cranny of the club and had taught himself how to connect the mains and fix the drainage; because he knew every member by name and everyone's salary; because he knew to the last decimal point the income and expenditure of the club on a day-to-day basis, there was nowhere to hide for anyone who was not completely on top of their job. Lloyd could tolerate honest mistakes and makes no attempt to hide how many he made himself, but sloppiness and lack of commitment took an employee straight to match point down and, with David serving, there was no way back.

But even lazy employees did not detonate the kind of fury Lloyd reserved for anyone he discovered cheating on him. 'One of the hardest things I had to accept in this business, especially in the beginning, was that people you thought were your friends stole from you,' he says, still conveying today the air of bewilderment at the thought of such a thing happening. 'They took things out of the pro shop and you wouldn't believe what went out the back door of the kitchen. The first year at Heston I lost £30,000 worth of toilet rolls. £30,000! I did the figures and I thought, "This can't be right!" How can you lose that much on toilet rolls! But it came to light when I started adding up some expenditure and thought, "I'm not making as much money as I should be here!" The membership was full; the money was coming in, everything looked great and yet there was something wrong. Those toilet rolls probably never arrived. Somebody knocked them off and just kept charging us. Unless you watch every item, it can happen at any time.'

But if that was surreptitious thievery, Lloyd ran into more blatant kinds head on. One day he was driving out of the front gate and a man emerged from around the fence with a plastic bag full of bark.

'He'd been stealing my bark right in front of my eyes! Tree bark from the mound in front of the club. It's expensive stuff, bark. And I thought, "How can he do this — he must have grown up in another country!" So I jump out of the car and chase him down the road. I caught him pretty quick because I was still fit in those days and took him to court and we won. Unbelievable stuff!'

One almost feels for the thief. The thought of being chased and caught by an indignant David Lloyd should be enough to straighten out many a crooked man. I suppose it is possible to argue with some of Lloyd's values, and it would certainly be possible to question some of his methods in the early days before success had been secured, but the principles by which he lives his life spring from an innate feeling of what he perceives to be right and wrong. They are not complicated principles because this is not a complicated man. What you put in is what you get out; work hard and you will be rewarded; loyalty is paramount; if you have a problem complain to my face; steal, shirk or shy away from your duty and you're out. It's all pretty simple.

But a lot of people couldn't handle it in those early days and Lloyd admits to an 80 per cent turnover in staff during the first year at Heston and not much less at some of his other London clubs.

'I was pretty difficult to work with at the beginning,' he admits candidly. 'I didn't listen very much and I just wanted to do everything myself. I didn't have a lot of patience with people who couldn't understand what I wanted. I suppose I tended to brush them aside and say, "Here, if you can't be bothered, get out of my way, I'll fix it." And that sort of attitude doesn't breed confidence in your staff. I was so obsessed with the whole deal that I learned everything about the place; every light socket; every pump; every bucket of balls; I knew where they were and how they should be used or could be fixed. That's good in one way because it keeps everyone on their toes if they know the boss knows everything that they know, but I probably could have been a bit more understanding.'

He won't find any of his friends springing to his defence on those self-directed charges. Roger Becker, Onny Parun, Donald Watt and even his brother Tony all witnessed what went on at Heston during the first couple of years and sometimes they cringed. Sometimes they got it in the ear themselves. But, believing in the man as they did and sharing his dream, they withstood the barrage and found that the storms passed as quickly as summer lightning. Lloyd is not a man to hold grudges. He has his say — sometimes too forcefully for some people's liking — and that is the end of it.

But some of the staff were not so resilient or forgiving and many left in high dudgeon. At that time in the Eighties, jobs were plentiful in the metropolitan area and many felt that they just didn't have to put up with it. 'London has always posed a special problem,' he says. 'Outside of London it is totally different. The provincial clubs have virtually no staff turnover. Glasgow's got almost the same staff as the day it opened and they're fantastic. I think the people outside of London have had it harder in the past and they appreciate a job more. If they get a job for £12,000 a year they know they are expected to put £12,000 worth of work in. In London they got spoiled, especially back in the early and mid-Eighties when we were starting at Heston. It is getting better now because everyone has been through hard times. But the only thing to do was to get rid of the ones that didn't fit and then start to build up a team of dedicated people with the accent on team work and team spirit. Part of the problem is that the very name of the job can attract the wrong sort of people. Leisure. They think, "Oh, wouldn't it be nice to have a cosy little job at a nice leisure club", and then they find out that it's bloody hard work. It really is a tough job dealing with the club members all day because they can be very demanding and sometimes very difficult. And so many people got a shock.'

Some reacted to the shock by smartening up and others were shown the door, although Lloyd discovered that firing people he considered incompetent or even dishonest was not as easy as he had imagined. Although the period has been increased to two years now, in the Eighties it was extremely difficult to fire anyone who had been in your employ for over a year. The law of the land was suggesting that if you had put up with them for a year you could put up with them forever.

'Before they changed it, you virtually had to have your hand in the till to get the sack,' he says.

But if the staff at Heston soon discovered that Lloyd's Law was every bit as stiff — if not stiffer — than the law of the land, then the members were left in very little doubt about it either. David busted a gut night and day to make sure that the club looked as good and was kept as clean as was humanly possible, and if the members abused the place they were left in no doubt as to how he felt about it.

A fair amount of money had been spent trying to make a former slice of wasteland in an industrial zone near London Airport look attractive, and one of the features David was most proud of was the large round flower bed that had been planted in the circle in front of the main entrance. So it is not difficult to imagine his rage when he drove in one day as the rain was teeming down to find a large, expensive car parked right across his daffodils.

'The bloody thing was parked slap on top of my beautiful flower bed. Ruined, it was. So I storm into the club and call out the registration number over the loudspeaker but no one comes. So I say, "Bloody hell, I'm going to find the bugger!" and I eventually track him down in the sauna. "I want to speak to you," I say. "I suggest you get some clothes on!" So he dresses and comes out and I say, "Your car! It's on my flower bed! And he gets all indignant and says, "You can't talk to me like that, I'm a member of Lloyd's!" And I said, "I don't care which Lloyd's you're a member of but you're definitely not a member of this one any more so please leave!" So he went. I couldn't handle that sort of stuff. I really couldn't.'

Even today Lloyd will not put up with bad behaviour from his members and encourages his managers to be as strict as he was. And in the Heston days, when he was on site day and night seven days a week (he reckons he gave himself one day off in the first 365), he was certainly strict. The night of the first club party, probably New Year's Eve 1983, he was doing his rounds to make sure everything was all right when he saw the lights were off in the little indoor pool area. Thinking there had been a fuse, he marched in and flicked the switch just to try it and found everyone splashing around in the nude.

'Stark naked, they all were. But not for long. They weren't members much longer, either. Starkers! I'd never seen anything like it!'

Desmond Lynam was not in there that night, of that you can be sure. But the unflappable BBC *Grandstand* presenter, who would probably remain totally unphased if a streaker ran through his studio, was just one of several well-known faces who played regularly at Heston during those early years. With Sue Barker introducing Cliff Richard, and Elton John making appearances for charity events, the club was not short of star quality — quite apart from international touring pros who used to drop by for practice whenever they were passing through London. Chris Evert practised there a great deal, as did Billie Jean King and Peter Fleming. And the Wimbledon doubles champions from down under, Peter McNamara and Paul McNamee, signed up as members sensing, rightly, that David's free hospitality was limited for anyone spending as much time in London as they did.

Desmond Lynam, in fact, was the first person other than the man himself ever to hit a ball on a David Lloyd court — quite a distinction considering that there are now 225 courts all over Britain.

'We were shooting a piece for *Nationwide* on the opening of the club and David seemed quite surprised when I got the first ball back to him,' Lynam recalled with a chuckle. ' "Oh, I didn't know you could hit a ball," he said, but of course I had always been a keen player and immediately agreed to sign up as a member when he told me a few months earlier about his plans to build a club. I must say I was sceptical at the time about its chances of success. But David's a robust character and he had the guts to go for it and make it work. It couldn't have been easy and I imagine he must have been pretty difficult to work for. But I had a great time in the early years because I had a bunch of pals who were also members and we used to get down there for a game two or three times a week.'

Quite a few of the early members were drawn from a disgruntled

1. The Lloyd Family practice a few strokes at Wimbledon. Tony tries out his backhand watched by John, David, and their parents, Doris and Dennis. (*Associated Newspapers Ltd*)

◀ 2. No mountain is too high…David scaling the cliff face at Berghead, north of Aberdeen during his days as a Barrett Boy.
(*Associated Newspapers Ltd*)

3. Time to polish the silver – David, Tony (centre) and John clean their growing collection at their home at Woodfield Road, Leigh-on-Sea. (*Ian Tyas, Keystone*)

4. George Worthington, the highly popular Australian who was coach to Britain's Davis Cup squad before his tragically early death, presents the Evening News Under 18 trophy to David at the Queen's Club after he had beaten Stephen Marks 6–4 6–4 in the final.
(*Associated Newspapers Ltd*)

16. Onny Parun, former New Zealand number one and now general manager at Heston, with two of his staff. (*R. Evans*)

17. Veronica Lloyd chats to friends while watching her husband captain the British Davis Cup team at the Castle Farm Club near Newcastle. (*R. Evans*)

18. A mixed doubles partnership that twice reached the Wimbledon quarter-finals re-unite during the 1996 Stella Artois Championships at the Queen's Club – David with Sue Barker. (*R. Evans*)

19. The final of the Gerulaitis Grassroots Challenge was played at Chigwell in 1996. Madras beat Kingston, Jamaica to win the trophy. (*R. Evans*)

group at the Queen's Club who were fed up with the increasingly antiquated facilities and were quite prepared to take the extra twenty minutes — or less if they were Italians in their fast cars as many were — to get out to Heston and its brightly designed indoor courts and modern sauna and jacuzzi. So far have we advanced in the intervening years that it is difficult to appreciate now that such items were considered rare luxuries in 1983 in England.

But although the emphasis has switched since, it was the tennis that set the standard in the early years, primarily because that was David's first love and his area of expertise. Generally unimpressed with the standard of coaching in Britain, he hand-picked the teaching pros to whom he rented court time and, whenever possible, brought in active players to bolster a teaching staff headed by his brother Tony and Donald Watt, who was still on the circuit himself when he agreed to embrace the Lloyd dream.

Onny Parun had been New Zealand No. 1 for many years in the Seventies when he had earned a deserved reputation as one of the workhorses of the old Grand Prix circuit; a player who extracted the maximum from his abilities and frequently beat more talented performers through fitness, stamina and dogged determination. In 1974 he had finished seventh in the Grand Prix standings, a position which earned him a place in the Masters which, that year, was played on grass at Kooyong in Melbourne. Parun led Bjorn Borg by a set and a break in the round robin before losing; served for the match against Vitas Gerulaitis and lost to Ilie Nastase. He was always pushing, pushing, forcing the best in the world to go that extra yard to beat him.

But by the early Eighties, Onny's career was starting to wind down and, far from being a dogged sort of bloke off court, he had become involved in the music writing business and various other improbable projects. Once, in 1979, when he was playing in the Queen's Club tournament, Onny ran into David Lloyd and heard about David's own project.

'He plonked down the plans for this club he wanted to build on the table in the restaurant and told me he'd be looking for people to come and help out,' says Parun. 'I thought, "Oh yeah, I've heard all this before." And I had, too. There was Jaime Fillol's club in Chile which ended up costing him a fortune, and Nikki Pilic was building one in Germany, and all sorts of other people were at it, so I just listened and wished him luck.'

Four years later, Parun was playing in Germany and, hearing Heston had opened, gave David a call. 'I told him I was thinking of passing through London and did he need anyone for a few weeks. I started working with Donald, charging about £9 an hour, and, although I continued to play the circuit a bit, I never really left.'

Today Onny Parun is Manager of Heston, having taken over in 1995 when the club started experiencing a few problems, largely due to the fact that, as the first one built, it is no longer the state of the art establishment that it was in the Eighties. Donald Watt, in charge at Glasgow, and Parun are the prime examples of Lloyd's philosophy of handing his teaching pros greater responsibility.

It did not take Parun long to start believing in David's dream. 'As soon as I saw what he was building and the energy he was putting into it, I knew he would succeed where others had failed,' said Parun. 'The very structure of the club is built to last. These are not flimsy buildings. The concrete uprights would withstand an earthquake. And the philosophy is sound. These are not clubs for snobs. These are places designed for normal families looking for value for money. And that's what we try to give them.'

Because he had to work so hard to compete with the best, Parun is no stranger to long hours, but even he has found the task of managing a David Lloyd Leisure Centre an exacting one.

'You don't get five minutes in the day to yourself, and the days never end,' he grins cheerily. 'Frankly there are times when I feel I'm overloaded. All day you are juggling different tasks, looking after the needs of 2,200 members, checking on maintenance, listening to staff problems and, as far as I am concerned, still getting out on court because some members expect that. But happily sometimes that is not possible because there are no courts available! Like today, I can't get a court inside so I am consigning myself to the bubble or maybe an outdoor court if the weather is not too bad because Bernie Levy, who has been a member here as long as I have been working at the club, wants a hit.'

The courts have been full virtually ever since Lloyd sat down after his first summer at Heston and decided that the original idea of charging £10 an hour per person for an indoor court with the outdoor courts free was turning him into a weather watcher with a bad attitude.

'I spent most of the summer praying for rain,' he remembers. 'It was the only way I was going to make money. So I decided to bite the bullet and up the monthly membership fees by £30 and let everyone play on any court for free. We got a few complaints, but then everyone came to accept it, and soon they were playing far more tennis because they forgot about the increase and began to regard tennis as a free item. In fact, they had merely paid up front and we had the money in the bank which is always a huge advantage for cash flow, quite apart from the fact that you make the staff's life easier because they are not counting as many pound notes and worrying whether someone has paid for their court.'

Although never a paid member of the staff, Charles Haswell was acting as a sort of unofficial PR man for the club and was responsible for organising many of the charity functions that took place there in the early years. Eventually in the summer of 1987 Charles pulled off his biggest coup by inviting the Princess of Wales to attend an exhibition aimed at raising funds for the Wishing Well Appeal which would benefit the refurbishment of the Great Ormond Street Hospital for Children. Boris Becker, Stefan Edberg, Pat Cash and Henri Leconte were star attractions from the tennis world, while David Frost compered the evening and Cliff Richard joined in some of the matches. To Haswell's considerable pride, the evening raised £240,000 — a record sum in England at the time for a one-night function.

Chapter 7

Sutton

It seemed like a great idea at the time, but sooner or later in this story of virtually unalloyed success, David Lloyd was going to make a wrong move; take a wrong turn; choose the wrong partner. Because of the kind of person he is, the club at Sutton, which was going to be the second jewel in the David Lloyd crown, was not a minor mistake. It was crippling. So crippling, in fact, that it brought the company's growth to a shuddering halt for the best part of five years and, had it not been for some very fast and pretty fancy footwork from Lloyd and his lawyers, it could have put the whole enterprise in a wheelchair for life.

With Heston showing a profit of £117,000 — far ahead of expectation — in its first year of operation, the search began immediately to find another suitable site. This duly materialised near Sutton, in an area close by the border with Croydon, that met all Lloyd's demographic specifications. The directors, who comprised Lloyd, John Barrett, Charles Haswell, Headley Baxter and the chairman Buzzer Hadingham, turned their attention to the need to fund the new project. They had all become close friends — Barrett and Baxter's relationship dating back many years — and every board meeting was preceded by a game of doubles, a happy ritual that continued when Hadingham had to resign on assuming the chairmanship of the All England Club. Baxter was a unanimous choice to succeed him as chairman of the company that, in those early days, went by the name of Willacre.

As so often happens, it was an introduction from a friend that produced the goods. Roger Becker knew a man called Richard Radin who had money of his own quite apart from having married into a Greek family called Economu which was anything but economic when it came to cash. Radin was a keen tennis player and had been looking for some means of investing in the leisure business. It seemed the perfect match. So a contract was duly signed between Willacre and Radin's company Hazelbaron which resulted in Willacre owning 15 per cent of a company that welcomed Lloyd and Baxter to its board of directors. The contract also included clauses that made Lloyd Managing Director of Hazelbaron with day-to-day control of the construction of the club. Radin was to be the provider of funds with voting rights but nothing else. No one need doubt that Lloyd made that very clear. His reputation as a man who insisted on running his own ship had already been well established at Heston.

'So we got started and everything was on schedule, but already I was starting to get a strange feeling about the partnership,' said Lloyd. 'Richard Radin had made some suggestions about the design of the club which we didn't think were right and we managed to skirt that. But then, on the days each week that I used to spend over at Heston, I'd come back to Sutton to find little things had been changed behind my back. Trivial things. Nothing you could make a big deal about but it made me anxious.'

The club duly opened in 1984 and Headley Baxter was installed as Manager. Both he and Barrett suggested that John MacDonald, a witty former New Zealand Davis Cup player, who had run World Championship Tennis on behalf of Lamar Hunt in Europe in the Seventies, be taken on as Marketing Manager. Johnny Mac's social skills were always good for morale and, for a time, it seemed as if the success of Heston was about to be repeated. So much so that talk soon turned to joining the two clubs and floating the company. The technicalities of doing so started with the need to find a base price from which to begin. It was obvious that there would be a variation in the percentage worth of Heston as opposed to Sutton in any planned merger, because the original club had been in existence for nearly two years and was already turning over a considerable profit while Sutton was in its infancy. But Lloyd did not want to get into any argument about it, so he suggested to both Baxter and Radin that they seek the services of Simon & Coates, brokers who were experts in the USM (Unlisted Securities Market) that was still functioning at the time.

'They came up with an evaluation which inevitably priced Heston higher than Sutton and Headley suddenly took the view that I was trying to screw Richard on the deal,' Lloyd remembers. 'I tried to point out that these were not my figures. That was what we had hired Simon & Coates for — to get an independent evaluation. I met with Headley and went over the documentation page by page, line by line. But he wasn't convinced and we had a hell of an argument. He then made some comments about me in the presence of Donald Watt and Steve Matthews which stunned them and which I found very difficult to forgive.'

It was clear by then that Radin was making it difficult for Lloyd to run the club the way he wanted. With Baxter in day-to-day control of operations, Radin became increasingly inclined to become involved with the internal affairs of the club. Lower-level staff were fired or promoted without proper procedures being followed and Radin's constant presence on site was confusing everyone. But to Lloyd's surprise and acute disappointment, Headley appeared to be settling ever more firmly on Radin's side of the fence.

John Barrett had a close-up view of what was happening and he was bemused. 'Headley had been such a close friend for so long I found it all very distressing,' he says. 'I just didn't agree with what Headley was doing and yet he seemed adamant. I had no hesitation in siding with David who had done absolutely nothing wrong and whose position was being undermined.'

It would have cost the Lloyd faction a great deal more had David been allowed to follow his gut instincts and let rip at a Hazelbaron board meeting which had been called ostensibly to issue a vote of no confidence in him as Managing Director.

'Here I have to hand it to our lawyers,' Lloyd smiles. 'I question their tactics and their fees often enough, but in this case they saved us. Given a free hand, I'd have gone into that meeting shouting and screaming even though I knew that, with Headley siding with Radin, there was no way I could win. But I was advised that if I refused to agree to anything, didn't talk, and just said "no" to every motion and proposal, they couldn't do anything. So that's what I did. There was no vote and within twenty-four hours I had issued orders to have my name removed from the club premises and resigned. There was no way I could fight the pair of them because I was outnumbered, but I wasn't going to have any motion of no confidence voted on my capabilities when I had done nothing to warrant it.'

Headley Baxter continued to run the Sutton club on Radin's behalf, and such were Lloyd's feelings about the matter that no one who considered themselves a friend of David dared be seen in the place.

'It all got a bit silly,' says Roger Becker. 'I live nearby and David came close to calling me a traitor for just using the facilities. Frankly, I wish I had never introduced Richard to David. It turned out to be the most embarrassing thing I've ever done.'

Lloyd admits that the episode stayed with him longer than most storms that have scudded across his volatile sky. 'It really hurt. Normally I forget an argument in a matter of hours. But this was different. It put us back four years in the development of the company. All we got out of the work we had put in to creating the club was the 15 per cent holding we had in Hazelbaron which they eventually bought from us. But personally it was much worse than that. Headley and I had been great friends. He had been my Davis Cup captain and had proved himself to be an incredibly hard worker both at Heston and Sutton I respected the man enormously. Then suddenly he is siding with a man I had no respect for. It was a tremendous shock and it taught me some hard lessons.'

Keen to get Headley's side of the story, I was warned that he had just undergone some very serious heart surgery after a routine check for a hip operation and it was some time before I could contact him. He eventually phoned, having just returned to England from a convalescent cruise in the Mediterranean. He sounded well and almost as robust as ever.

'Listen, I know why you have been calling and I really don't want to dig up the past,' he said. 'A long time ago David and I had a business disagreement. I can go off the handle and so can he. It got a bit out of hand and ended up being very bitter which was sad. I had some money in the company but there were other shareholders and I wasn't in complete control. But that's in the past. Things can never be quite the same between us but we talk to each other again now and I've congratulated him on being Davis Cup captain and I think he'll do a bloody good job.'

Headley described himself as being on permanent holiday now, happy to have survived a life-threatening operation. He spoke of David being lucky, not to put him down because he also noted his 'terrific pride and determination', but just in the sense that everyone who has been as successful as his former partner needs luck. It was almost wistful although Headley, tall, dapper and handsome, has too much pride himself to be caught at that game. His directness, laced with humour and charm, make for a very compelling cocktail. Like David and JB, I just find it all incredibly sad.

Insight II

Motivation

'In the beginning, we didn't have good training programmes. We just expected people to get on with it. I thought "training?" Surely, everyone should know what to do. Shove someone in and say, "Right, get on with it." But I was wrong. It was one of my big mistakes. You have got to give them the background to the job; explain why they need to do things a certain way. You can't fire someone for screwing up when they haven't been told what it is they are supposed to be doing. That's wrong.

'We didn't spend nearly enough money on training early on and I'd still like to see us spending more now. But motivation is not only about training. It's about building a team and injecting team spirit into that team. Making them feel part of something; literally give them a stake in it. Right from the start Midland Montague and I agreed that shares of the same price should be offered to the staff and several took them up. Then we offered share option schemes, and those that have been with me since the beginning — there must be about sixty or seventy of them — have built up quite a shareholding which is great. It's important to give them part of the action and make them feel part of the business. We encourage them with all sorts of rewards and keep them as involved as we can. They are all part of the puzzle that makes this company tick. I take the accolades because it's my name on the door, but it isn't me. I've got a hell of a team and you can't do it without them. And it's important for them to know that and to reward them.'

Chapter 8

Finchley

By the time Finchley opened, David Lloyd was able to get through a speech without the tears. In fact, so confident was he of the viability of the company that he was building, that he stood up and made a couple of heavy political points in front of the only political audience that mattered in 1989 — Prime Minister Margaret Thatcher.

Finchley was the Prime Minister's constituency and she had not needed a great deal of persuasion to open a club built on the private enterprise principles that had been the bedrock of her political philosophy. It helped, too, that she had known the Lloyd family for some time as her daughter Carol had written a book several years before on John and Chrissie. However, she might not have been anticipating a little lecture over interest rates but that was what she got.

'I said that I felt Nigel Lawson, who was Chancellor of the Exchequer at the time, had to be very careful about interest rates if the government was not going to run into problems. Small businesses were already being hurt and they were supposed to be a prime concern for the Conservative Party. In the end I was proved right but Maggie was very good that day and showed that she had been listening to everything I said by replying to my speech point by point. Then she walked around talking to people, chatting away, being very professional in her attitude to the occasion and I was very impressed. She remained a member and often used to come back for tea parties and things like that which gave the club a terrific boost.'

For tennis enthusiasts in north London, the David Lloyd Club at Finchley seemed almost too good to be true. The Cumberland Club near Swiss Cottage had been the great gathering point for the serious players in that area of town for decades, but there were no indoor facilities and the long winter months were full of frustration.

Barbara Dein, the American wife of the Arsenal Vice-Chairman David Dein, had always been a keen player and, like many other active women in the area, jumped at the chance to sign up for membership.

'It was great to have somewhere warm and comfortable to play in those damp winter months,' Barbara recalls. 'And when I saw the creche where the mothers could leave their children while they played or went off to shop, I was really jealous! My boys were grown up by then and I thought, "Oh, how I could have done with something like that when they were little!"'

Barbara Dein now plays most of her tennis at the Queen's Club where she is a member of the women's team. 'I have a lot of friends there and the facilities at Queen's have improved so much in recent years.'

David Lloyd realises that and is not being unduly boastful when he points to the root cause of the rapid improvement at Queen's. 'We forced them to improve,' he says. 'They were just stagnating before because there was nowhere else to play. They had a captive membership. Then they started to see their members join Heston in droves and knew they had to pull their socks up. Some smaller clubs have complained when we have opened up in their area, but we have never hurt clubs that are any good. Connaught, which is not far from Chigwell and Cumberland, has simply got better as a result of us being around. People should welcome competition. Those that can't handle it shouldn't be in business.'

There were the usual queues of people lining up for membership forms when Finchley held their open day prior to the Prime Minister's visit. Once again Lloyd was taken by surprise at the response, but he was not getting carried away by the idea of people flinging money at him. One extraordinary incident showed him just how important it was to stick to one's principles and not allow rules to be bent.

It had been decided to open Finchley as a non-smoking club which seemed like a good idea at the time but, in fact, has not been followed as a rigid policy at subsequent clubs.

'We have very well designated smoking areas set aside at our other places because we found that, if you ban smoking altogether, people just go into the lavatories and put their cigarettes out on the floor. It was incredible. The floors were ruined. So we had to make a very small area eventually at Finchley where people could have a puff if they were desperate. But we wouldn't change the basic no-smoking rule because that was the premise on which the club was opened and we felt we had to stick to it.'

Even, as it turned out, in the face of considerable temptation. Lloyd was walking around making sure the membership applications were going smoothly when one of his young helpers came over to him in a bit of fluster. She had been approached by a man who not only wanted to buy a life membership for himself but also for three of his family. At £6,000 each that came to a nice little twenty-four grand — all of which he had in cash in a suitcase!

'You'd be amazed how many people pay for life memberships in cash,' says Lloyd. 'Normally we are quite happy to take their money but on this occasion there were strings attached. This chap had told the girl that he had the money and was ready to join but that he didn't like the no-smoking rule. "If you can waive that rule, then I'd be happy to have my family join," he had said, standing there with this case bulging with notes. So I went up to him and said that we couldn't break the rule under any circumstances. "It's not the way we work here," I explained and he said, "Well, that's it, then" and walked out. It was tough watching all that money walking down the path but I never regretted it. If you make rules, you just have to abide by them. Otherwise we would have been advertising under false pretences. In the end it was the behaviour of the members who did join that persuaded us to set aside one small room for the smokers but that's a situation which evolves and forces you to take a certain action. We certainly weren't going to be bribed into it.'

Finchley, with its updated design and prime location, was an immediate success and provided the impetus for the building spree that was to follow in 1992 when Lloyd defied everyone's advice and opened three clubs virtually at once — Bushey, Chigwell and Enfield Just to add to the expansion, the Ten-Pin Bowling section was also added to Raynes Park.

Young managers were starting to take over the day-to-day running of the clubs as Lloyd saw the inevitability of having to stand back a bit and be less hands-on. Some were tennis pros like Donald Watt and Steve Matthews who quickly benefited from David's refusal to stereotype people.

'That's one of the most infuriating things about the corporate structure, the way it pigeon-holes staff and sets them on a ladder on which they are supposed to progress rung by rung at the prescribed pace. If someone is better than someone else, there should be room for them to leapfrog. If they have a variety of skills, they should be allowed to move from one department to another. You should never be allowed to hold merit back but companies do. "Oh, he's a bit young, we can't have him. He might do something the CEO doesn't like." That sort of attitude is appalling. Young people should be given a chance to prove how good they can be. That's one of the great satisfactions of running a company like this — spotting untried talent and giving it the opportunity to blossom. I do it on instinct. I'm a hopeless interviewer. I never know what questions to ask and usually find I have made up my mind within a few minutes of the person sitting down in front of me. It's something about a person's attitude and manner which tells me all I need to know. I've been wrong a few times but not that often.'

Nikki Baker was one of the young people to benefit from Lloyd's liberal promotion policy. A South African who had started her career as a teacher and played hockey to county level, Nikki was also well versed in computers by the time she applied for a job with DL Leisure. And with an outgoing personality to match all her other qualifications, she was quickly taken on board. She is now manager of Finchley and Bushey which were merged into one club as far as membership was concerned and has already successfully demonstrated the new-found flexibility of Lloyd's management style.

Lloyd is the first to admit that it takes a brave person to stand up and argue their case at one of the frequent open meetings he conducts with his managers. But, nonetheless, he encourages them to do so.

'They'll say, "David, I don't think you're right, we've got to do it this way", and I'll argue and argue in defence of my point of view. But if they stick with it and present a rational case, I'll tell them to go away and prove it. If they turn out to be right and it benefits their club, I'm delighted.'

Nikki Baker stood up at one meeting and insisted that the menu they were offering at Finchley and Bushey was not right and could be significantly upgraded.

'I thought we could price up,' she says. 'I felt we needed to offer the members better quality food and that they would be willing to pay just a little bit more for it. David disagreed. He felt we would price ourselves out of business in the restaurant, but I stuck to my guns and eventually he gave in.'

When Lloyd saw that Baker was determined and had done her homework on the figures he said, 'Well, I don't think you're right but you deserve a shot at it. I'll give you six months to prove me wrong.'

And she did. The response at both clubs was very favourable and by the end of her test period revenue was £3,000 a month up.

'Obviously it was satisfying for us to have achieved that and it gave you confidence to try other things,' says Nikki. 'The challenge is always there and the members keep you on your toes because they can be quite critical. The two clubs under my responsibility are not far apart but have separate identities with Finchley being heavily tennis-orientated — we have 80–85 per cent court usage — while Bushey has a fantastic gym that just heaves. But everything has David's stamp on it. He has put his heart and soul into these clubs and it shows. People love it when he drops by which he still does regularly. You can watch members quickly dreaming up some reason to go over and have a chat with him, often with a complaint about something or other, but if it's reasonable, he'll always listen. You even get kids asking for his autograph. It's definitely a special company to work for and David's the main reason for that.'

Assessments like that, which can be found from staff members throughout the company, will leave those who didn't last the course at Heston in the early days scratching their heads in disbelief. This was not quite the David Lloyd they knew.

Chapter 9

Chigwell

The opening of Chigwell took David Lloyd Leisure into East Enders territory. Relatively wealthy East Enders to be sure, but certainly a somewhat different crowd from the members at Finchley and Bushey. The differences, as one Jewish journalist wrote, between bagels and cream cheese and bacon sandwiches. Members who like their mobile phones so much that everyone swears that one day a member playing on Court 4 phoned the guy playing on Court 2 to ask for his ball back — and got an answer!

Once again Lloyd turned to someone he could trust to run the place, and once again it was a tennis pro, someone in fact who had worked with him for a spell in Canada. John Marnoch, who is still captain of the Essex county team, is reasonably well versed in the lifestyle of Essex Man, but on the very first day he found himself having to deal with the quirks of Essex Woman. Sitting in his office, wondering whether the caterers had got the stock lists right and whether the showers would work, Marnoch was suddenly confronted by a woman who opened the conversation in promising style.

'I've got a complaint,' she said.

'Oh,' replied Marnoch nervously, not daring to imagine what was coming next. 'What's wrong?'

'I was in the pool and I got my hair wet!'

Hang on a minute, thought Marnoch, she's having me on here.

'This chap was swimming up and down and splashed my hair!'

'It wasn't Mark Spitz, was it?' replies Marnoch who was now convinced the woman was joking.

'I don't know the member's name,' she replied stiffly. 'But I never wear a cap and I've never got my hair wet before. It's disgraceful!'

Poor Marnoch didn't have a solution to that problem but he

learned fast and managed to head off a potentially serious problem that arose not long afterwards. This time a female member accused a man of dropping his trunks when they were in the pool together and there was no one else around. So Marnoch called the man in and confronted him with the accusation. Not surprisingly he received a flat denial. So after talking over the problem with David, he called them both into his office and said, 'Look, I don't know what happened because I wasn't there. But as it is your word against his, there is no way to resolve it unless you agree to put the matter behind you and forget it. The only other solution is for you both to leave the club.' Without much hesitation, they shook hands and stayed.

But Marnoch suffered greater and more prolonged abuse from another man who has also, strangely, declined to remove himself from the membership lists. The problem started when the fellow saw his shiny new BMW convertible being driven out of the parking lot with the guy in the driving seat waving to him.

'The first I knew about it, the guy was going bananas at the reception desk, screaming blue murder at everyone,' recalls Marnoch. 'I could understand him being a bit upset but he was determined to hold me responsible and kept up the barrage of abuse for two weeks. By that time I had contacted the police who had put a tracer on it. As a result the car was found parked outside a finance company in Southend. Apparently he had omitted to pay his monthly instalments on the car for the previous seven months — just about as long as he had had it. He wasn't too happy when I told him where he could find it.'

What had occurred was a classic 'snatch-back' — the method by which companies who are owed fortunes by forgetful clients reclaim cars that are not being paid for. The finance company employees had been able to pull it off because the member had left his car keys at the desk — a practice which has now been discontinued.

Marnoch was promoted from Tennis Director to Club Manager when Mary Collins moved to Enfield five years ago. He confirms the recent trend of a rise in health and fitness members as opposed to full membership which he attributes primarily to the cost factor for families.

'A full family membership which just includes husband and wife runs to £78 a month after a joining fee of £450. Then, if you have two children, each costs £14 a month which pushes the monthly bill up to £106. Yet you can have a health and fitness family membership for £62 so there are definite savings there.'

Like all the other managers I spoke to, Marnoch is in awe of David Lloyd's work ethic. 'When I was in Canada with him, he worked unbelievably long hours and put so much into the junior programmes he supervised,' says Marnoch. 'I've got some talented boys here at Chigwell but they don't know what hard work is. I have to kick them out of the lounge sometimes. They think two hours on court is a day's work.'

Some of the Chigwell members got a close-up view of what some boys can achieve when Marnoch answered my eleventh hour call to stage the final of the Gerulaitis Grassroots Challenge at his club on the Sunday prior to Wimbledon this year. The Challenge, named in memory of Vitas Gerulaitis who helped me get the original Brixton vs Harlem matches started in the early Eighties when he and Peter Fishbach had masterminded a major inner city tennis programme in New York, consists of eight teams drawn from cities around the world comprising two boys between the ages of thirteen and sixteen. For the past two years, we have held the event at Spitalfields, under the roof of the old vegetable market opposite Liverpool Street Station. But Market Sports, which runs five-a-side soccer on its indoor courts, could not accommodate us for the final day so I asked Marnoch if we could use his facilities. 'No problem. What do you need?' was his immediate response. We needed a court, some balls, an umpire and some sandwiches, all of which was provided with a cheery smile by Barry Lees, the duty manager. Madras won the tournament for the second consecutive year after a closely fought final against Kingston, Jamaica with players from the other teams — Belfast, Los Angeles, Melbourne, New York, Soweto and Philadelphia — acting as ball boys. The standard of tennis was high and I will be very surprised if Vijay Kannan from the Britannia/Amritraj school in Madras does not go on to distinguish himself on the pro tour. I hope the Chigwell members at least had a glimpse of what we are trying to achieve. The interaction of kids of that age from vastly differing backgrounds is a joy to watch because it is so easy and uncomplicated. They were friends in twenty-four hours — black and white, Hindu, Christian or uncommitted. It didn't seem to matter: tennis was their lingua franca and for most of them, who had never been on a plane before, the experience transcended what happened on court. But they loved the club and David Lloyd is keen to help us get involved in more grassroots schemes. There is so much more to be done.

Insert 3

Jubilation

'I tell you one thing I share with John McEnroe — the pride in representing my country. A lot of big-name American players have blown hot and cold over the Davis Cup and I've never understood that. But McEnroe was always there, no matter how difficult the assignment, until they got on his case and suspended him.

But the jubilation of winning for your country is as big a thrill as I have come across in my sporting career. The most overwhelming experience of this was after the doubles in the Davis Cup tie against Italy in 1976. You can read about, in detail elsewhere but to have been in such a classically hopeless situation — two matches down in the tie, two sets to love down, match points down — and to have pulled it all back in front of an unusually partisan British crowd who were going absolutely wild on Wimbledon's No. 1 Court — well, it still gives me goosepimples to think about it.'

Chapter 10

Veronica

Housed in one of the spacious, modern offices at the Arena, head-quarters of the David Lloyd Leisure Group, a small company called Design Collective represents the latest product of a union that has now been in existence for twenty-four years. The earlier, somewhat more important products were called Scott, Camilla and Laura — the Lloyd's three children whose ages, twenty-one, seventeen and fourteen suggest a well-planned family.

Until its director hired an assistant late last year, Design Collective was a one-woman company; a formalisation of a job that Veronica Lloyd had acquired by default all the way back prior to the open of Heston.

'We need furniture,' David had announced as if hit with an original thought. As he was looking at his wife at the time and showed no inclination to prolong the conversation, Veronica assumed that she had just been assigned to go and buy some.

'David wasn't interested in doing it,' Veronica explains. 'He was all caught up with his figures and problems with the builders, banks and local council so I thought I had better get on with it.'

One senses that Veronica is very good at getting on with things. For a start she is Scottish; a Glasgow girl from a notable family who veils a briskly determined and efficient nature behind a shy exterior. Almost timid, in fact, until you catch a glimpse of the sky blue eyes. Then you sense that this is a woman who knew what she wanted fairly early in life and, having made her choice, has not spent much time regretting it.

'No,' she says in a soft voice that still carries traces of her heritage, 'there has not been a dull day, really.'

The days would not have been particularly dull even before she first set eyes on a young tennis player at a junior tournament at Exmouth in Devon when she was just fourteen. Back home in Glasgow, Veronica was one of four children of Cochran Keith MacLennan who had risen through the ranks of one of Scotland's most celebrated companies to become Managing Director of Robertson & Baxter, purveyors of such malts and whiskies as Cutty Sark. As for most children from affluent backgrounds in Scotland, tennis was part of the curriculum, but two of MacLennan's girls showed a greater aptitude for the sport than most. Veronica was good enough to play in junior tournaments all over Britain and was seeded at Junior Wimbledon in 1965, but her elder sister Frances was a bit better than that. After leaving Millfield, a great tennis school at the time, she rose to be No. 1 in Scotland and, as a long-time member of Britain's top ten, played extensively on the international circuit in the Sixties.

To an even greater extent than her sister, Frances was a young lady of independent inclination, and when she set eyes on Roger Taylor she did precisely what Veronica was to do and fell in love with a tennis player. Undeterred by the fact that Taylor, a steelworker's son from Sheffield, did not quite match her social standing or that, as one of the most handsome and desirable male athletes of his generation, Roger was pursued, not always unwillingly, by virtually every airline hostess who tried to fill his coffee cup while gazing into his eyes, Frances got her man. It was rarely an easy relationship and eventually foundered during the difficult days, many years later, when Taylor was trying to maintain the initial success of the club at Val do Lobo in the Algarve which bore his name.

A brother, Keith, who has four children, has remained in Glasgow where he works for his father's old firm, but the most remarkable member of the MacLennan offspring is undoubtedly the oldest sister Lindsey who is a professor of medicine and is credited with developing the ultrasound process by which heart problems can be detected in unborn children. Now living with her second husband in Ridgewood, New Jersey, Lindsey travels extensively, lecturing at medical conferences all over the world.

After the first glimpse at Exmouth, Veronica and David did not start seeing each other seriously for another five years, but the relationship developed quickly and they were married in Glasgow in 1972. It was right after Veronica got her degree from Glasgow University in psychology and politics, either of which would have helped her deal with the temperament of the mercurial personality she was marrying. Although the bride probably had her mind on other things on the wedding day, Dennis, with his impish sense of humour, best remembers the fact that his middle son couldn't get his top hat on.

'John's head was too bloody big!' he says with a roar of laughter. 'Couldn't find a hat to fit him. He had all that hair at the time, too. Eventually we did a swop with my son-in-law, Bob Hammond, but it still looked like a pimple stuck on top of his head.'

Having played tennis herself, Veronica knew what she was letting herself in for by marrying one of this strange breed of self-driven, nomadic athletes who plied their trade all over the globe. Inevitably David frequently had to travel on his own because there was precious little money in the pro game in the Seventies for anyone who did not warrant a place on one of the three World Championship Tennis tours that Lamar Hunt was funding. Under the direction of Mike Davies, the former British No. 1, there were three tours of thirty-two players each and Roger Taylor and Mark Cox were the only British players who came close to joining a hierarchy which, in retrospect, seems even more daunting than it did at the time. Ken Rosewall, Rod Laver, Bjorn Borg, Roy Emerson, John Newcombe, Arthur Ashe, Stan Smith, Cliff Drysdale . . . this was company David Lloyd was never destined to keep on court.

The alternative in those days was the fledgling Grand Prix circuit, devised by Jack Kramer and Donald Dell and run under the auspices of the ITF, that included the likes of Jimmy Connors and Ilie Nastase but did not require players to be signed to professional contracts as was the case with WCT. So there were tournaments of varying size and strength, many of them dotted around the traditional watering holes of the European game like Monte Carlo, Baden-Baden, Barcelona and Hamburg. Partly because of cost and partly because David never went near a plane if he could help it, the Lloyds travelled to many of these events by car; ferreting out cheap hotels and hoping the tournament directors would provide at least one meal a day at the club.

Soon Scott had arrived and he quickly filled up the back seat of the car. The baby evidently became so accustomed and soothed by car travel that when he started crying in the evening, David had to take him for a spin. 'Once round the block did it,' he recalls. 'Out like a light!'

But the nomadic lifestyle never appealed to Veronica very much and she was soon spending more time at home, bringing up the children and experimenting with the basic job of furnishing a house. Although she could not have realised it at the time, it was good preparation for what lay ahead.

After sojourns in Holland and Canada, the Lloyds settled back in England at their house in Claygate, not far from their present home in Oxshott, and the club idea began to form. Dennis Lloyd had always managed to leave his business life in the City and talked about other things (tennis, inevitably, being the primary topic) when he got home. But there was no chance of David being able to switch off a mind that was in overdrive for most of his waking hours.

'I always knew everything David was working on because he always talked to me,' says Veronica. 'I knew everything and the children knew everything. It was impossible not to, really. And I became heavily involved in Heston because, in the beginning, there was only him and me. There was no staff. And so, although I was not technically qualified to do anything in particular, by the time the actual building was about to end, we started to think about how we were going to furnish the place. After looking at a couple of places we were both pretty shocked at what was being suggested, so David just said, "Go on, you do it." '

Once again, refusing to do things by the book ended up enhancing David Lloyd's business. The big furniture houses, when confronted by this young lady wanting to furnish her husband's leisure centre, all clicked into their pre-conceived notion of what a leisure centre looked like — steel fittings, spartan, utilitarian — and came up with everything that the Lloyds didn't want. 'It was amazing how difficult it was to get people away from their fixed image of a leisure centre,' says Veronica. 'Even today, after we have hopefully provided a few alternative examples, there are those who just don't get it. We wanted a more welcoming, comfortable feel; more like a hotel lobby, perhaps. So I just started looking around and picking out what I liked. I still do and that means we chop and change a lot, but there are some companies that I still do business with now, thirteen years on, because they have proved to be the best — companies like Brinton's Carpets from Kidderminster, a very old-established firm who have never fallen below the standards they set themselves long ago. Scottish leather manufacturers like Andrew Muirhead are also people I deal with regularly because we are using more and more leather, not just because it has a luxurious feel about it but because it wears well and is easy to clean. But otherwise I experiment a lot and am always looking for different suppliers. I get yelled at for that because everyone tells me that it would be much more economical if we did the same thing again and again. But that would be very boring. Obviously if we standardised, we could use the same furniture supplier but, funny as it may seem, clubs develop their own feel and personality and what looks good in one frequently wouldn't look good in another. And, anyway, I have made lots of mistakes and it would be stupid to keep repeating those mistakes. You learn something with every club.'

In the beginning, the budget was tight and, inevitably, the furniture was cheaper. But now Veronica is able to go for better quality materials and that, in itself, turns out to be a money saver. She would not, for instance, have opted for the bamboo chairs and tables that were being used at the Castle Farm club in Newcastle during the Davis Cup against Slovenia. Not because bamboo is not durable as far as the main shafts are concerned but because things unravel at the seams.

'Look,' she said picking at a piece of bamboo binding that had broken on the back of a chair. 'It starts to look terrible eventually. But as we didn't build this club from scratch, we have inherited a lot of things and it will take time to change them.'

There are, of course, considerable advantages for a company that is sprouting branches all over Britain in having one person who can look at it as one diversified entity and who knows, literally, where every chair and piece of curtain material is to be found. Although Veronica tends not to mix and match very much, there are occasions when a whole stack of furniture is put on a lorry and ferried the length of the country.

'We did that with some small tables and chairs that were not being used at Glasgow. Reading was in need, so we moved them down there. But the good thing now is that I work so much more closely with the architect so that we are actually discussing things like door frames and which types of wood to use before the place is finished. At the start I just sort of came along and furnished the club when the architects had moved out, but it is much more rewarding to be working as part of a team.'

Ever since the rush of openings with Enfield, Finchley and Chigwell in the early Nineties, being the design director at David Lloyd Leisure has become a full-time job for Veronica and it obviously gives her a great deal of satisfaction to contribute so fully and creatively to her husband's venture. But, like David, she finds the comments on her work come in the form of a complaint far more often than they do as praise.

'Some of the members are a little difficult to please,' she says diplomatically. 'At some of the clubs, a lot of people don't know who I am so I stand around the bar sometimes and listen to the comments. And they shock me. Several times I have heard people say, "Oh, they don't care, they fill the place up with any old thing just so long as it doesn't affect the profit margin." I am left speechless by that sort of comment, which is probably a good thing. If only they knew how much effort we put into it — sitting around the kitchen table at home, working out colour schemes and trying to decide what would look best. That's the disheartening part. But you've just got to get on with it and hope that the majority of members approve.'

Chapter 11

Beckenham

If you drive a few hundred yards past the big white house with the blue car parked in the courtyard, you come to one of the driveway entrances to the Beckenham Place Park Golf Club. The house is noteworthy because the car carries the number plate 1 NGB which could be broadly translated as Nigel Benn is No. 1. Not too much hype about that because, of course, Benn has been middleweight champion of the world.

The house no doubt cost a fortune as, indeed, do many others in this exclusive enclave of opulent homes which rings the outer fringes of the Park and its meandering golf course. Ironic, in a way, because it represents the only place — other than the Sutton fiasco — in which David Lloyd has lost, if not quite a fortune, then at least a serious amount of money.

There are two issues at stake here. Firstly, Lloyd wanted to build a leisure centre in a largely unused field. That will now never happen. Secondly, he deviated from his normal method of doing business in various ways. He ventured into golf and, in addition, agreed to act purely in a managerial role for property he did not own — in this instance for the actual golf course which is used by two clubs, Beckenham Place Park and Braeside, as well as by the public. This he still does, although at the time of writing, it was far from certain how long he would continue to do so as the four-year lease had only one year to run.

Those are the bare facts of a saga that speaks volumes for governmental stupidity, bureaucratic incompetence and local residential intransigence and fear, all fuelled by rumour and innuendo. It led to David Lloyd being abused at meetings, challenged by window-thumping motor cyclists on motorways, and accused of some seriously hilarious crimes. On the basis that it is better to laugh than cry, John Cleese ought to be brought in to write the script. There is a sequel here to be called 'Fawlty Parks'.

Let us start with the attempt to build another leisure centre. Following his dictum of 'location, location, location', Lloyd thought he had found the ideal place. Although it is appallingly signposted from the South Circular, Beckenham is a densely populated suburb close to Crystal Palace and not far from Croydon. If you turn off the main road and enter the old posthouse gates to the park and drive down Foxgrove Avenue, it is not long before you pass one of the major sporting complexes in south London — the Beckenham Tennis, Hockey and Bowls Club which is the site of the annual pre-Wimbledon grass court tennis tournament. It is a private members' club and provides just about everything you could wish for from an upmarket English style (i.e. non-luxurious) establishment except the two items DL Leisure specialises in — fully equipped gymnasiums and indoor tennis courts.

Continue on down a steep hill and the road eventually peters out just before the tiny Ravensbourne railway station. Twenty yards before the station entrance, the road turns into a bumpy, unpaved, pot-holed thoroughfare that made me happy the suspension on my Fiat would be Hertz's problem and not mine. Fifty yards farther on you can turn left at the beginning of a fenced-off council estate and almost immediately find yourself at the entrance to what is called Summer House Field. Just inside the gate there is a large rectangle with a few bricks and bits of charred rubbish lying on it. That, until July 1995, was the Summer House. In an act of vandalism so senseless that one instinctively searches for ulterior motives, it was set alight and burnt to the ground by a bunch of kids from the estate across the shaded lane. No one I have spoken to has suggested that there is any connection between the fire and the fierce, not to say deranged, opposition that had been building up against David Lloyd's plans. There are indeed reasons why this would seem far-fetched as the timing is a bit off — building permission had already been denied — and it was not the council estate residents who were objecting to the project but the owners of the expensive houses farther up the road. Nevertheless, it adds another strange twist to an already strange tale.

Apart from anything else, it provided a sad end to a three-storey pavilion-type structure that had been built in 1900. Originally it was the headquarters of the Ludgate Circus Gentlemen's Sports Club, a wondrous title which immediately conjures up images of moustached gents in straw boaters with old school ties holding up their trousers. If the place is secluded now, it must have been a real hideaway in 1900 and one can only speculate at what un-Victorian activities the gentlemen got up to after stumps had been drawn. Later, it was taken over by Thomas Cooke's and eventually bought by the Lewisham Council in 1978. The Council used it for their weekend cricket leagues for several years, but it fell into a state of virtual disuse by 1993 and was just waiting for the kind of saviour David Lloyd could have become.

Many of the local residents viewed him somewhat differently, however. Less saviour and more devil incarnate. So convinced were they that he was going to ruin their way of life that a 'Save Beckenham Place Park Campaign' was launched with extraordinary vigour. The main complaint was over the planning permission he had applied for to build a club on Summer House Field. But there were also objections over his alleged plans to upgrade the golf course and its stunning 300-year-old Manor House which acts as the clubhouse and which, as Paul Hanks of Lewisham Council readily agrees, is in desperate need of restoration.

People were convinced he was going to ruin the Manor House, even though it is a Grade Two listed building which means that you can't so much as put an inter-connecting door in an existing wall. Everything has to be restored under the eagle eye of the National Trust, so there was absolutely no chance of Lloyd being allowed to ruin it. All he was doing, in fact, was trying to save it — a job reckoned to require expenditure of £750,000 according to an independent survey carried out on Lloyd's behalf. He was prepared to invest that kind of money in the place on condition he got planning permission for the club at the bottom of the golf course and received a long lease from the Council to manage the course. Four years with a two-year option did not quite do it.

'Nobody in their right minds would pour that kind of money into

123

a place only to risk being thrown out after six years,' says Lloyd. 'The Council has now increased that to ten but even that is too short. Anyone who restricts leases to that sort of length of time has no conception about building a business over the long term and investment management. You can't do a proper job in that length of time and you certainly can't make money out of it, so where's the benefit? It's crazy.'

Possibly not quite as crazy as the more fanatical members of the 'Save Beckenham Place Park Campaign', whose tentacles, to David's amazement, reached far and wide. Steve Matthews, who now runs the Raynes Park club, was in Brighton for a day at the time and saw people leaving the local Tesco being asked to sign a Save the Park sheet.

'In Brighton, for heaven's sake!' exclaims David, who is still exasperated at the memory of it all. 'But it didn't stop there. One day I was driving back from Heston, coming down the A312 to Hampton Court, and I'm waiting there in the traffic, about to turn left down to the river, when I see this guy on a motor bike with a big, black helmet on coming down the river so I stop to let him pass. Instead, he stops and bashes on my side window, yanks his helmet off and screams at me. "You're going to destroy Beckenham Place Park! Save Beckenham Place Park!" Then he puts his helmet on again and roars off. Unbelievable! Bloody unbelievable!'

Even that was not quite as unbelievable as the poisoned dog story which really did bring everything into John Cleese territory. At about this time, Lloyd took Ian Taylor out to Beckenham to show him what a private investigator had already determined — that Summer House Field was not only invisible to all the houses in the vicinity but was probably the most underused stretch of land in the entire Lewisham Council area. In two weeks of non-stop observation by a man positioned at the edge of the field, a total of precisely fifty-five people (plus almost as many dogs) had walked across it. Lloyd was wanting to create a centre where 700 people would use it daily.

But that was not going to happen, ultimately because one man was given the power to say no and used it, but also because of the fear factor. While David was strolling a few yards away, a woman with a dog fell into conversation with Taylor and soon mentioned

Lloyd's name.

'It's terrible isn't it, what he's doing,' she said. 'Really shocking!'

'What's that?' asked Taylor.

'Oh, haven't you heard? He's poisoning our dogs!'

Needless to say, this was too much for David. Having overheard this conversation, he strode up to her and said, 'Excuse me, madam, but I am Mr Lloyd and although I'm not a big dog fan, I certainly have no intention of poisoning your animals!'

It is the oldest political trick in the game, of course. Find out what really scares people and then convince them your opponent is going to make it happen. Enoch Powell became a master of the art with his speech on immigration in the Sixties and Pat Buchanan made full use of the tactic during his attempts to beat Bob Dole in the race for the 1996 Republican nomination in America. A whispered aside to a community's leading gossip and a rumour will catch fire faster than the time it took to burn down the Summer House.

'It was absolutely amazing and actually rather scary,' says Lloyd. 'Steve Matthews lives not far from there and he did a bit of under-cover work for me, pretending he was one of them and listening to what they were saying. Some of the things that were being said were unbelievable and had nothing to do with saving Beckenham Place Park. The people down the end of the line signing petitions weren't really told the proper story at all. Some of them honestly believed I was going to poison dogs. Someone must have told them that. It was wicked. They said I was going to do all sorts of things I had no intention of doing such as raising the membership to £3,000 a year.

'Even during the course of two weeks of public meetings, when we showed them membership forms with the projected price on them, they still refused to believe us. We gave presentations outlin-ing exactly what we were going to do and they yelled back, "Oh, no, you're not going to do that!" and I said, "Yes, we are and we can show you what we've done at other clubs to prove it." But they didn't want to know. It was all negative, negative and really abusive as well. But unfortunately that's just the way some people are.'

Steve Matthews had an even more hair-raising view of how some people allow themselves to become completely carried away by an issue that hardly warrants such emotion.

'On one occasion, David had to cancel a scheduled meeting and the three hundred or so anti-Lloyd campaigners who had been preparing to give him a rough time decided to stay on and have a council of war. At first they thought I was one of them so I sat back and listened in amazement as they listed all these things they intended to do like start a smear campaign in the press and get the rumours going about poisoning the dogs. Then suddenly someone noticed my David Lloyd plastic membership card, which I had hanging on my key chain, and they sussed out who I was. So I decided to get the hell out of there as fast as possible but even so some guys started chasing me and I only just made it all the way down to Catford Station ahead of them. I'm sure they would have given me a rough time had they caught me.'

It was no better when David did turn up for a meeting. Chairs were thrown at him on the stage and when the meeting was over an elderly lady walked up to him and, in all seriousness, said, 'If I were a man I would shoot you!'

Matthews, who witnessed the scene, was aghast. 'And all because she thought she would no longer be able to walk her dog! Are people completely out of their minds?'

Despite all of that, Lloyd came closer to getting the go-ahead for a club on Summer House Field than many local residents dared think about. As usual he prepared his campaign well. The field in question was not green belt and David would not have bothered if it had been.

'We never go for green belt, you can't win no matter what the circumstances are. It was what is called "white land" which means that the inspector appointed by the Department of the Environment has the right to approve it.'

But in this case he didn't. Despite the fact that Lloyd offered free use of the club to those householders in the immediate vicinity, discounts for others in the Beckenham Park area, an extra nine holes added on to the existing golf course, a promise to pave the pot-holed road leading from Ravensbourne Station and, of course, the considerable benefit accrued from jobs, the answer was a resounding "No!" Not even the prospect of creating jobs impressed the Inspector. Two hundred people are employed on the building of a

DL Leisure Centre and some seventy are taken on full-time after opening. Many of these could have come from the adjacent estate which would have improved some people's lives and, just conceivably, helped cut the crime rate.

None of this was sufficient to win the approval of the better-off residents in their nice homes. To them a paved road with a big club at the end of it would only mean more traffic and an end to their little exclusive cul-de-sac with its discreet railway link to the city. It was a perfectly natural reaction and, viewed through their narrow prism, a justifiable one. What was not justified was the length of time it took the Inspector to come to a decision after Lewisham Council had accepted Lloyd's argument and given their own stamp of approval.

'Lewisham wanted it, but the D of E still insisted on having a hearing. Two years we waited for the hearing. Two years! And then they handed it over to the Inspector to make the decision entirely on his own. He writes a report, sends it to John Gummer's office and, if it is not overruled, his decision stands. I understand Gummer intervenes in less than 10 per cent of the cases so we had little chance. So the Inspectors are given incredible power even though, in this case, I believe the guy was unqualified to pass the sort of judgement that was required as he did not appear to have any serious interest in sport. He said it was not acceptable to build a club in open space even though that field is completely invisible to everyone except passengers in the trains that pass down one side of it.

'He refused to accept the arguments we had put in two other cases where we had met similar opposition. At Raynes Park and Chigwell, our barrister argued that a club like this was simply sport with a roof over it. Not a supermarket. Not an office block. Just outdoor sports with a roof. We won two appeals like that but not at Beckenham. It was knocked back and cost hundreds of jobs and a fantastic facility for the local people to enjoy. And it cost us a tidy sum, too. A minimum of £120,000, certainly.'

Whatever your viewpoint, no one can argue with David over the placement of the field and its usage. When Stefan Brewster, the assistant pro shop manager up at the Golf Club, and I arrived, one woman and her dog were leaving. When we left, a man and his dog appeared from the distant adjoining field behind some trees. Otherwise Summer House Field was left to ghosts of those sporting fellows from the Ludgate Circus Gentlemen's Sports Club — and maybe their ladies. And it is invisible until you actually walk through the gate. Not a single house overlooks the place. Just the trains.

There are probably a few ghosts lurking around the old Manor House, too. It certainly has an eerily familiar feel to anyone who has been subjected to the damp chill of an English public school when you walk through the front door and the impressive colonnade. Immediately on entering, a visitor finds himself in a good-sized, windowless room with a high ceiling. Part of the room nearest the door is partitioned off in a haphazard sort of way by a wobbly wooden contraption standing about two feet high, which looks ridiculously at odds with the faded grandeur of its surroundings. The grandeur fades instantly, however, on entering the wash-room area. Here one is plunged into a dank, dripping world of stained basins, taps that don't work and cisterns that won't flush. Dennis Lloyd would have recognised it immediately from his days in the army. In the Forties and Fifties, Britain was full of toilet facilities like this. The place reeked of everything that David Lloyd had banished for people joining one of his sports clubs.

So why did it exist at an establishment managed by David Lloyd Leisure? The reason is as straightforward as the circumstances are complicated. DLL has allocated a limited budget for maintenance on the Manor House because no company in its right mind is going to spend the millions of pounds needed here on a property they do not own and on which they cannot obtain a lease of more than six years. The particular washroom in question appeared to be that part of the building allocated to Braeside Golf Club to judge by the members' lists and tournament results pinned to a noticeboard on the wall. No doubt members had complained. But it was the same old story that has kept sports clubs in a state of genteel or not so genteel disrepair for years — members won't pay high enough fees to generate proper income and local councils won't allow management companies leases of sufficient length to turn a long-term profit. The result is bad-smelling drains.

Braeside has been in existence since 1947, the year a group of Beckenham Place Park members broke away to form their own club. According to Trevor Moorcroft, Hon. Secretary of Beckenham Place Park, the two clubs 'co-exist now', as he puts it, which suggests a bit of flack flew around for some time.

Moorcroft is justifiably proud of the fact that Beckenham Place Park shares a birthdate of 1924 with Augusta, Georgia and, although his course is never going to be in danger of bearing comparison with the manicured magnificence of that used for the Masters, he insists that it is a fine course which could be vastly improved with proper funding. And that, of course, is where David Lloyd comes in.

You have to leave through the front door again and work your way around the side of the building before arriving at areas of the building that DLL has renovated. The cramped but well-stocked Pro Shop is one and the new bar and restaurant is another. These areas and the course are run by Huw Davies Thomas who was brought in by Lloyd after the pair had met at La Manga in Spain where Davies Thomas was working.

'We've done what we can with the amount of money that David has made available but it's very frustrating,' says Davies Thomas. 'There is so much that needs to be done. The potential here is fantastic but the house is very old and requires a great deal spent on it. Given a realistic lease David would spend the money. But all that is up for discussion yet again with Lewisham Council. New people have moved in to the relevant decision-making positions so we are just going to have to wait.'

Meanwhile the taps drip . . .

Insight 4

Negotiation

'I'm afraid I don't have a great deal of tolerance with haggling when I negotiate a deal. I want the proper price up front, first time. But it is incredibly difficult to get people to do that. I've been in meetings in the City where some guy takes a bit of paper and says, "Well, let's see, the price will be . . . de-dee-de-dum . . . £50,000", and you can see he's picking numbers out of the air. So I say, "How about £25,000?" But what is this? I just want to know the proper price, if there is such a thing. It's the same with building contracts. They start giving me all this crap and I say, "Are you going to build this place or not? Don't fart around. I'm not going to negotiate. You're not going to come back later and say you want something off the price. I want the right number now. Bottom price." I'm going to go to the guy with the best offer and deal with a straight hand. I'm not going to have someone come in the back door and say, "Whatever they say, we'll match it minus fifty." That can't be right. It's not fair and it just creates more work. I don't understand why people aren't honest from the beginning.

'I know what my maximum price can be from the start. I've done my figures. If the price goes up we have to cut spending. And they try to get you to do that by saying, "Just cut out a couple of tennis courts." But if I do that it would cost me three hundred members. I can't cut the facilities because that's my income. Some of them don't see that and still try and get clever with prices. It's frightening how people seem incapable of taking a direct route through a problem and say what they mean. It would save so much time.'

130

Chapter 12

Flotation

There are very few pictures on the wall of the chairman's office at the Arena but one of them is of a horse. Its name is Sound Man and it is a winner which is appropriate because it is named for David Lloyd. One senses there are few things that have tickled David's fancy more than having this horse named after him by his Irish friends, as he calls them. Or to be more specific, Denis Brosnan and his pals in the Irish bloodstock industry. They constitute a group who know how to live life to the full, and when they were looking for investment in England, they found a soulmate in the tennis-playing entrepreneur with an eye for good odds and a winning ticket.

Brosnan wears many hats. Chairman of the Irish Horseracing Authority, he also heads up the Kerry Group, an international food company and was brought in as chairman of Leisure Holdings plc, a company funded by bloodstock money and formed in 1988 to capitalise on the new trend towards exercise, health and fitness. By the summer of 1990, Leisure Holdings were looking for investment in the UK. David Lloyd Leisure was not only the pre-eminent outfit in the field, but its young chairman was also on the look-out for backers. He had plans on the drawing board for three more clubs, but he needed heavy funding and Brosnan had the money. The two men hit it off immediately, and by October Lloyd had somewhat surprised himself by feeling quite good about a deal that gave Leisure Holdings 58 per cent of his company in return for £10 million and made Brosnan chairman of his board.

'It just felt right,' Lloyd explained. 'I liked them instantly and knew that they weren't interested in trying to tell me how to run my business. Nevertheless we spent a lot of time together and I thoroughly enjoyed my visits to Ireland. They have a zest for life which I find immensely appealing.' Owen McGartol, Chief Executive of Leisure Holdings, is quick to let you know the feeling is mutual. 'We had a very happy relationship with David,' he told me from his Dublin office. 'Most of us are self-made men just like he is, and there was a mutual respect from the word go. We got to know all his top people over in the UK and realised that they were a very dedicated group with a tremendous sense of loyalty to David.'

Bolstered by Leisure Holding's funds, Lloyd was able to go ahead and open three clubs at Chigwell, Bushey and Enfield in January 1992, giving the company an impetus which has never slowed.

'A little later we took a combined decision to float the company,' says McGartol. 'And it turned out brilliantly. It was oversubscribed six times from day one and we came away with a handsome profit. But that did not end our relationship with David. The social links continued and I think he was pleased when we decided to pick a really good National Hunt horse and name it Sound Man as a tribute to the way we think of him. David has a stake in the horse and I think he enjoys it.'

That would be something of an understatement. To watch David at a racecourse on the day his steed is running is to see someone having the time of his life. Like a kid let loose in a candy store, he can be seen rushing from the paddock to the bookies and back again, thumbing wads of notes, checking form and listening intently to every pearl of wisdom that falls from the lips of the experts.

'Normally I never carry any money,' he laughs. 'But when I go racing I need it! It's an incredible industry and nothing is left to chance, nothing. You wouldn't believe the extent to which everything is planned down to the last detail, from the breeding to the winner's enclosure. It's an exhilarating sport and my Irish friends certainly know how to make the most of it.'

The FLOAT

David Lloyd had first met David Cohen in 1986. Heston was a reality; just about everything else was still little more than a twinkle in Lloyd's eye. Cohen, a small, sharp, sandy-haired stockbroker, had many of Lloyd's qualities. He was competitive; he was enthusiastic and he knew his business. The two men liked each other on sight and the tennis player turned entrepreneur looked instinctively to Cohen for advice. He wanted to know more about the City and how it worked. He knew it held the key to the future success of his enterprise. His friend Terry Eccles at J. P. Morgan had taught him about merchant banking, and now he needed to understand the Stock Exchange and shares and how to raise large sums of money.

Lloyd and Cohen flirted for a time with the idea of joining the Unlisted Securities Market which existed at the time. Making what Cohen describes as a lucky decision, they dropped the idea just a matter of weeks before the October crash of 1987. His little empire intact and bolstered by his new Irish partners, Lloyd and Brosnan began thinking seriously of floating the company towards the end of 1992. There were eight units by that time with Glasgow under construction. Money was needed all the time to keep moving ahead and occasionally he got lucky. Plans were set to expand Raynes Park by adding a Bowling Club. It would cost £1.3 million. This time he did not have to look very far. Brosnan suggested he talk to Francesca Welbore Ker who was a director of Leisure Holdings and therefore also sat on the board of DL Leisure. If people are made directors of companies so that they can lob over a million or two whenever needed, then Ms Welbore Ker fitted her role perfectly. She produced the £1.3 million as a bridging loan with no guarantees. No wonder David loved the Irish. However Lloyd's board was not overladen with ladies with such deep purses and generous dispositions. A million or two was nice but much more was needed if the startling progress of the previous two years was to be maintained.

'There was sufficient profit and a sufficiently strong management structure under David by then to make flotation a realistic option,' explains Cohen. 'The earnings outlook was excellent. Pre-tax profit had been increasing steadily year by year from £600,000 in 1990 to £2.5 million in 1991 and £3 million a year later. The momentum was there.'

Cohen, who has since moved to Société Générale in Broadgate, was with Robert Fleming at the time and agreed to work with David on a prospectus that ended up being 110 pages long. 'It took a lot of bolting together,' says Cohen. 'By March 1993 we had a document that was the result of some very intensive work. We wanted it to act as a marketing tool, but it also had to include full accounting balance sheets and, at the end, detailed coverage of all the legal aspects. We spent a lot of time on the glossy cover, too, trying to get the balance right.'

Then the two Davids put on their hats and coats and, as Cohen puts it, 'went tramping around the City'; knocking on doors and showing their prospectus with its slides and drafts to such institutions as Legal & General, Morgan Grenfell, Schroeder's and Guardian Royal Exchange. They held a meeting with 160 fund managers and felt the pulse of the City. Gaining a consensus of opinion is all part of the preparation for a flotation, and Cohen was determined to come up with the right numbers.

'It was an arduous business,' admits Lloyd. 'I don't know how many meetings we sat through, and without David and Ian Taylor to help me through it I would have been suicidal.'

But Cohen was enjoying it. Managing a good float was what he did best and it engaged all his business acumen and intellectual powers.

'There were different aspects to this, too, which made it interesting,' he says. 'First of all there was David. He may have been impatient with some of the legal niceties and inclined to blow his top over a few of the clauses, but he had wonderful input. I learned never to underestimate David Lloyd. He may not have had a very long formal education but there is a great business mind inside that head.

'Then there was the fact that a huge percentage of existing shares came onto the market. I was handling 39 million shares out of a total of 46.9 million. That's 83 per cent when, with most flotations, it doesn't get much higher than 25 per cent. In all 29,363,280 existing shares were sold and ten million new ones raised to fund the company.'

But there was plenty of drama before all that happened. On the day of the flotation, about twenty people gathered under the Scottish paintings that line the magnificent boardroom at Robert Fleming's City offices and Lloyd was in about the same state as he would have been sitting in the Centre Court waiting room at Wimbledon. It was getting near match time when Cohen would present to the board his estimated price at which the shares should be floated.

Cohen's job requires an absolute knowledge of market forces; how they will react and what they will allow. Mark them too high and the market will react badly. Mark them too low and the price will soar, leaving the shareholders feeling ripped off. It is all a question of delicate balance.

'Any fool can sell a pound for eighty pence,' says Cohen. 'It's a question of whether you can sell one for three pence higher, or maybe four. It all depends on what you are selling and the mood of the City towards that kind of stock at the time.'

The tension mounted as the lawyer went through all the legalities of the float, dotting every 'i' and crossing every 't', while Lloyd squirmed in his seat. To break the monotony, board members started laying wagers on the price range they thought Cohen would come up with.

'I was optimistic and went quite high in the range we were anticipating which was between £45 and £55 a share,' says Lloyd. 'The betting got quite brisk but the lawyer was still talking, asking me infuriating things like, "Could I prove I owned my name?" He was doing a very good, thorough job but I thought, "I can't stand this" and I lost my temper with the guy. He was trying to cover every eventuality, which is right, I suppose, but some of the things he was droning on about had less chance of happening than an earthquake splitting Throgmorton Street. So finally I get him out of there and David Cohen comes in as the last notes are changing hands under the table.'

Cohen laughs at that. 'I knew there was some betting going on and, knowing that group, I was pretty sure it wasn't a couple of fivers, either.'

Leisure Holdings had a lot more riding on it than a bet or two. While David was the only member of the board who intended to hold onto every one of his shares after the float, the Irish were planning to sell all theirs, all £45 million of them. Eyes swivelled towards Cohen as he came into the room.

'Well, having gauged the market as best I can,' Cohen began, glancing around the room at the expectant faces, 'I think the proper price to pitch this at would be £67.'

For a second, there was dead silence as everyone struggled to make sure they had heard him correctly.

'Oh, is that all you can manage?' asked Lloyd laconically before everyone broke into huge grins.

'In fact David had got it absolutely right,' says Lloyd. 'It was brilliant. Put into multiples that came out at a flat £1.50. The perfect float is a share that moves up 10 per cent when it is put on the market. Then everyone is happy.'

A week later, when the shares would be traded on the Stock Exchange for the first time, Cohen took David, Veronica, Scott and Lorna Browne, the company secretary, along to watch the name of David Lloyd Leisure go up on the big board. Everyone held their breath when the shares started trading and immediately went from £1.50 to £1.65.

Cohen was just as excited as his visitors. It was his work, after all, and, had something strange happened, it would have been his reputation on the line. 'I was thrilled when they didn't shoot up right away,' he said. 'That's not good for anyone in the long run. We had achieved the classic 10 per cent mark-up that you are always aiming for. The Irish were pleased because I had pitched the price higher than they had anticipated so they came away with four or five million more than they bargained for. And David was delighted when the shares he still retained gradually went on climbing to around the £1.85 mark within a few months and then, of course, shot up to £4 at the time of the Whitbread takeover.'

The City had taken a little while to get used to this tennis player with his flashy Ferrari. David did not quite fit the pin-stripe image that goes with the company Jaguar.

'One would never call David ostentatious but he does have this weakness for expensive cars,' Cohen said, laughing at the memory. 'He had one of those bright red Ferraris at the time which are absolutely unmissable and attract a lot of attention. I used to get colleagues dropping comments about the fact that my client had parked his machine smack in the middle of Throgmorton Street and how was business? It was impossible to have a meeting with David without everyone knowing he was there.

'There was also the time when I took a minibus load of fund managers off to have a look at a couple of his clubs. I suggested that, as he would not want to give the impression that he was beyond the need of any funding, he might ditch the Ferrari for the day and maybe borrow someone's Vauxhall. Anyway we arrived at Enfield and the Ferrari was nowhere to be seen. We were then moving on to Chigwell and David said he would follow. All went well until we were drawing up at some traffic lights on the North Circular and, in the rear view mirror, I see this little speck of red getting rapidly larger. Suddenly, with a whoosh, he draws up in the lane right alongside us with all our fund managers staring at this red monster and David's little face peering up sheepishly from his low-slung seat. It was amazing we got any money out of them at all.'

Even after the float, analysts still needed convincing even though there were a few who could see from the financial reports that something positive was going on in the leisure industry. Mark Finney at Nat West was one of those who were curious enough to want to see first hand what a David Lloyd Leisure Centre looked like.

'Basically I had no idea what to expect,' Finney told me from his Edinburgh office. 'I remember very clearly driving out to have a look at the club at Bushey one Tuesday morning. It was about five months after the flotation, which had gone well, but I still wanted to have a first-hand look. Frankly I didn't expect to see too much right off. I thought it might be a quiet moment to look around. But when we arrived we couldn't get into the car park! On a Tuesday morning! I suppose that was the moment I got really excited about the whole concept. I realised then that we might be on to a winner.'

The next thing that impressed Finney was the range of facilities available. As he pointed out, there had been swimming pools before, and tennis clubs and gymnasiums, too, but no one had tried to put all of them together in such an attractive package.

'This whole leisure idea had been something that people in this country had sort of half felt they needed for some time,' Finney continued. 'But bringing a lifestyle change in from the States is always about timing and, either by luck or design, David judged his moment perfectly. Even with him building clubs at the rate he is, it is still an undersupplied market but of course from now on it will become increasingly competitive.'

At Nat West in London, Susan Noble, another analyst working in the leisure division, is as bullish on the David Lloyd concept as Finney.

'People may have thought he had a potty idea originally but David Lloyd is very much liked in the City now,' she says. 'Basically, David created a new market that simply was not there before. Now all sorts of people are trying to jump on the bandwagon. But we got excited about the stock very soon after the flotation in 1993. When a stock is recommended we have five different gradings which in ascending order are: 1. An outright buy. 2. An add. 3. A hold. 4. A reduce. 5. A sell. For one of the smaller companies coming to the market for the first time it is very unusual for them to be graded for an outright sell straightaway but that is what happened with David Lloyd Leisure. It is rare because there is a higher risk ratio with what is basically an untried concept and you always get the negative factor of people not believing in it. But that was never the case with David's company.'

Chapter 13

Glasgow

Glasgow was another gamble, in its way as daring as the first venture at Heston or the insistence on opening three clubs virtually at once in 1992. Glasgow was a gamble not just because it was Glasgow, which was dubious enough in itself, but because it took David Lloyd Leisure outside the cosy, proven confines of Greater London.

By 1993 even the most negative critics of David's dream had to concede that the concept worked in those hand-picked suburban areas of London which were either in or within reach of the affluent stockbroker belt. But there was still huge scepticism about how well it would work farther afield. And Scotland! Lloyd was warned by everyone he met about the Scots, many of them overlooking the fact that he was married to one!

'I was told to beware of Scotland,' he recalls. 'I was told they were mean and didn't spend money the way other people did — not even those who had money and there is no shortage of it around Glasgow. And even when we did open, people said, "How can you manage a club in Glasgow when you live in London?" And I told them firstly because I had a great manager on site and secondly because I could hop on a shuttle and be at the club in about the same time as it took me to drive round the bloody M25 to Finchley!'

He is not exaggerating. The Glasgow club, which is actually situated in Renfrew, is to be found at the gates of Glasgow Airport. Once again location was a primary consideration. As it sits at the end of a motorway, everyone not only knew where it was but were confident that they could get there quickly. Even so, people had reservations, including many of David's friends.

Harry Matheson, a former Scottish No. 1 who is married to the former British player, Carole Rosser, knows the habits of his country's sporting community as well as anyone. From his post as manager of one of the leading sporting goods stores in the city, Matheson has a good ear for local opinion and even he wasn't convinced.

'We knew there was a need — no question about that,' says Matheson. 'But neither Carole nor myself were sure it would work. You have to understand the mentality of the people up here and the kind of grudging acceptance that nothing terrific is going to happen. The idea of a multi-million pound tennis club with all the modern facilities being built on our doorstep was just a little difficult to take in. And then there was the question: would people pay for it?'

On the first Open Day, when the place was a building site and it was pouring with that kind of icy rain that Scotland seems to patent, two thousand people showed up with money in their hands.

'It was bloody unbelievable!' said Lloyd. 'They were buying memberships on the spot. We always have an Open Day about four months prior to the actual opening and give people a 50 per cent discount on the joining fee if they like what they see and agree to sign up there and then. You have to have imagination to understand what the finished product is going to be like because four months ahead of time it looks a mess. You point to a hole in the ground and say, "That's the swimming pool." You need a leap of the imagination, especially on a lousy day. But we try and make it as welcoming as possible with free wine, some of it served hot, and tea and coffee and they come in droves. At least they always had done in London but this was Glasgow and we didn't know what was going to happen. The response was amazing.'

The response was in answer to another mail drop of the kind that David had first tried at Heston. By the time the Renfrew club was being built, the system had been streamlined to the extent that his organisation just dealt with one central agent as so many local newspaper shops are now owned by the big chains like W. H. Smith or Menzies.*

*Being a good Glaswegian, Veronica Lloyd pronounces Menzies the proper way which is difficult to catch phonetically but sounds closer to Mengis. As a child, she remembers 'old Joe' Menzies, as he was known, having an office near her father's in Glasgow.

'It was an incredibly good deal,' says Lloyd. 'It cost us just £8 per thousand papers to carry the insert plus about £1,200 for the printing. We spent about £2,000 and drew 2,000 people. It's tough to beat that.'

If you can manage to entice 2,000 people to your site before there is anything to see, word of mouth becomes your next best advertising medium. But Lloyd leaves nothing to chance and Glasgow was hit with a commercial radio blitz as opening day approached. The result exceeded everyone's expectations and even a sceptical financial analyst, sent up secretly to see what this crazy tennis player who had floated his company on the stock market was really up to, came away with his eyes bulging.

'As soon as Glasgow was successful, we went through the roof from the point of view of market perception,' says Lloyd. 'Then, they really did start to believe in the product because it wasn't just luck. We had proved it could work, not just in London but elsewhere, and that we could run it. But, I tell you, it hadn't been easy. Once again so many people had been negative. In Britain, everybody down the line — sport, business, whatever — they always look for the bad points, the down side. Always, always, always. It drives me mad. In America, it's the other way. Too much the other way. But there has to be a happy medium somewhere. The only answer is to keep being positive and drive forward; just keep going no matter what people are telling you. Many of them want you to fail for whatever reason. Personally I don't understand it. Instead of thinking, "Oh, this is great!" they just want to know how much money you've made. So you've made some money. What's that got to do with it? I admire them because they've been successful at something that was probably difficult to achieve. Tennis players are no better than anyone else. It used to be different in the days of the great Aussies like Lew Hoad and Roy Emerson but basically everyone is jealous and afraid of everyone else's success. They're so insecure. It's just the same in business, maybe even more so because there's not even a sporting element to it. Although I've been very lucky in most of the people I have dealt with, there are some very negative people in the City. That's why I can understand people like Richard Branson who have bought their companies back. I can really understand why he did that. We were just lucky — the people I dealt with loved the concept.'

Donald Watt basically loved the concept, too, but still found himself taking a deep breath on occasion as David Lloyd led him into yet another adventure. Watt was a good tennis player who was failing to make it in the big time when Lloyd hauled him in from the cold the year Heston opened. Watt is a handsome man with an attractive Scottish burr in his voice who made friends easily during his coaching days at Heston and was suddenly presented with an extraordinary opportunity about a year before Glasgow was due to open. Elton John asked him to become his personal, private coach. On the road, all expenses paid for him and his wife plus a salary that was three times what he had been getting at Heston. And he rarely had to work more than two hours a day!

Lloyd had already earmarked him as manager for Glasgow — with his background he was the obvious choice — and saw no reason to stand in Watt's way when Donald asked him for a year's sabbatical. If that could be taken as a test of Lloyd's man management he passed it with flying colours. Had he refused, he would have sent Watt to Glasgow wondering what might have been. Instead Watt returned to his new, expanded role in the company with money in the bank and an unforgettable experience to look back on. Better still, he was not only refreshed by the change of pace but, more importantly, he had seen that he needed more satisfaction from life than hitting with a strictly moderate tennis player for an hour or so every morning and then spending the rest of the day by the pool in some exotic hotel in Los Angeles, Hong Kong, Buenos Aires or Rio.

'I wouldn't have missed it for the world,' says Watt. 'But the fact that Elton is a great guy and treated us unbelievably well just wasn't enough. After a couple of months, one just lay in the sun and wondered if there shouldn't be a bit more to life. For Elton, of course, it was great. He was on tour and I was there to give him his exercise every morning at a sport he truly loves. But apart from the thrill of being able to attend some really major Elton John concerts around the world, and having a look at the inside of the pop music business, the appeal of the lifestyle was limited.'

It has been said that a Scot only returns home to collect his brother but in this instance Donald Watt turned up in Glasgow so sated with the good life that he welcomed the raw, misty morning with spartan glee. It was not as if he, too, had not had his doubts when he had returned to Edinburgh to visit his parents a year before and had then driven over to Renfrew which, by chance, was his wife's home town.

'I had only been there once before to see her cousins and, this time, David had warned me I would be coming back to manage the new club and had told me where it would be located. I remember staring out over the site on a bitter winter's day and I couldn't even see where the courts would be. It was scary. I thought, I'm coming to this? But then I reminded myself that David had been right at every stage along the way so I just went off with Elton and hoped he'd be right again!'

Watt and the Lloyd family went back a long way. He was a contemporary of Tony Lloyd's and had stayed in John's flat in Wimbledon at odd periods, the way young players do as they camp out with friends in between foreign trips. But it had been at the West of Scotland tournament that he had first run into David.

'I can remember as if it was yesterday. He was playing the tournament and was also involved in some sort of promotion for Red Hackle whisky which was one of the companies Veronica's father ran. I saw him again on a satellite circuit in Holland and then, one day at the All England Club, he told me that he was building a tennis centre out at Heston. He was direct as usual. He said I was obviously struggling to make it on the pro tour and would I go and work for him? He didn't expect an answer right then but just told me to keep in touch. That was in 1980 sometime. In March or April the following year, I did as he suggested and met with him at a little office he had at the time in Hammersmith. "We're opening in September," he said. "You'd better get down here a month before." Just like that. Then he drove me out to see the site and I'll never forget how he laid it all out for me as we headed out to Heathrow. He said how this was going to be the first and then he would have clubs ringed all the way round London. He saw it all. Looking back now, it's scary. And he talked about getting Slazenger involved with a squad of kids and then, of course, he set up the Slater scheme which ultimately produced Tim Henman and Jamie Delgado. Talk about vision and making your dreams come true!'

Nobody has had a longer, closer look at the way David Lloyd operates than Donald Watt. He has been there since day one, surviving the staffing eruptions and disruptions of the early years when family members were rounded up to fill in for employees who had quit or been summarily fired and being questioned once or twice on his own dedication to the cause. We were talking in Watt's small office at the Renfrew club after Lloyd, who was visiting for the day, had shown me round the premises. I asked Donald if he had ever come close to getting fired himself.

'Not seriously, I don't think,' he replied. 'But there were a couple of times . . . well, I was twenty-one and a tennis pro and I got involved with a couple of women over that period and maybe I'd come in at nine in the morning instead of seven and David would have me in and ask what was affecting my work. Basically he was wanting to know why I was no longer there fourteen hours a day, seven days a week. It would have been impertinent for most bosses to ask but with him, how could you object? Not only was he working longer hours than you but he was incredibly loyal. A couple of times as duty manager at Heston I'd have run-ins with members and you might say the wrong thing. But I always felt that, being a tennis player, I was a little bit like him and got volatile at times and he always backed me 100 per cent. And it's the same today. The manager of each club is the manager of that unit and he will back you to the hilt. You'd have to physically hit someone for him to seriously question your motives. That's because he doesn't appoint people he doesn't trust. And in the old days it had to be mutual trust. I never had a contract, everything was done on a handshake. But watch out if you don't return the loyalty. He can be brutal. Especially in the early days when he had everything on the line — his house, the lot — he could blow up and then it was really fearsome.'

Many, of course, couldn't handle the heat and — often quite literally — got out of the kitchen, convinced that David Lloyd was a raging maniac who was impossible to work for. But Watt was amongst those who understood what Lloyd was going through;

what he was trying to achieve and how little experience he had in trying to achieve it. And, inevitably, those who survived found themselves being conditioned to the Lloyd work rate and work ethic.

'It rubs off,' Watt agrees. 'I come in in the morning and I look at the bins outside and make sure the back gate is shut. I check to see the vents are OK. I know what he'd be looking for. I find myself picking things up at the club that I don't pick up at home and my wife makes me feel guilty when she says I care more about this place than I care about the house. But if you've worked for David for a long time, you just start thinking that way and there's no chance of you ever forgetting it. He was picking up bits of paper as soon as he walked in here this morning and when he noticed some broken glass in a corner he said, "What's going on?" '

But worse was to follow that afternoon. As has been noted, Lloyd has always been sceptical about the cost-effectiveness of security guards. He accepts them as a tedious necessity, viewing them as an item on his balance sheet that rarely offers a proper return for money — like lawyers. But Glasgow has an excellent head of security, Harry Lyons. The trouble was that the very day Lloyd chose to visit the club this particular week was Harry's day off. And when David walked through the car park just after lunch, the deputy was to be found in a parked car, with his feet up, fast asleep.

'And the guy had only been on duty two hours!' said Lloyd, his voice rising to that high-pitched level of exasperated indignation. It was, of course, the last kip the guy took on David Lloyd's property and his security forces had even more ground to make up in the eyes of their boss.

There are ten tennis courts at Renfrew with a new tennis hall just added, but the activity which greets a visitor on a midweek afternoon in April is all concentrated on the fitness machines. There are 186 of them at the last count and many are lined up alongside the indoor swimming pool. Due to modern heating technology, the canopy over the pool can create a temperature of 26.5°C (80°F) for those swimming, while the guy sweating on the exercise bike two yards away is peddling in 12.5°C (55°F) — all in open space. As has happened at Heston and other clubs, extra room has been created for fitness machines to meet the demand. David Lloyd Leisure is, in fact, now the biggest buyer of these contraptions in the world which ensures Lloyd a very warm welcome when he turns up at the industry's world trade fair in San Diego, California each year.

There he can select from a full range of torture machines that would make the most dedicated masochist grimace with pleasure. A company called Life Fitness supplies the cycling contraptions that are becoming increasingly high-powered in a computerised sort of way. Then there are the Cybex weight machines and the Verca Climber that Martina Navratilova loved so much. All these machines are becoming more sophisticated with each passing year. Soon there will be a card that can be swiped through a selected bike that will give the machine all your height and weight specifications and adjust itself accordingly. But, more than anything, Life Fitness and Cybex equipment has to be sturdily made. Usage can run up to sixteen hours a day, not all of it gentle. But Watt recognises, as do the other club managers, that fitness has become the core of their business and good maintenance is paramount. And not only maintenance. Replacement is also a none too infrequent occurrence, especially after Lloyd has cast his eagle eye around what is available from the state of the art stalls at the San Diego Show.

Lloyd took some of his best performing managers with him last time — part of a bonus perk that would see them end up at the Hyatt Grand Champions at Indian Wells hitting balls into the Californian desert for a few days — and Watt was amused but not surprised to see David place his order for the new Life Fitness bikes. The bill for Renfrew alone came to £150,000.

'Typical David,' said Donald when I spoke to him a month after the trip. ' "I want them NOW", he said and sure enough they arrived today, right on time.'

Manufacturers who recognise a good customer when they see one tend not to mess around with people like David Lloyd, especially in America where service is considered a competitive tool. And so Watt had just spent the day installing a new range of bikes that were all styled in the racing position so that even the flabbiest member could dream on as he or she set out on their own personal Tour de France from a static position by the swimming pool. They cost £3,000 each and no wonder. All are equipped with, amongst other little gems of computerised information that many of us would rather not know about, a heart pulse machine that uses a strap around the chest to monitor your heart rate with every push on the peddle. All go with the arteries. And if it doesn't look as if it is going to be all go, at least you get a chance to stop before the heart does. Very comforting!

No wonder all this high-tech wizardry is attracting members by the bike load, but it is interesting to hear Watt maintain that tennis is still the key to the success of the whole venture.

'There are, of course, clubs in the group like Reading that opened purely as fitness centres, and they have been successful too. But here tennis is the key. It is what attracts people in the first place. Then they come and see the gym and they're overwhelmed by the sheer scale of what we have going here. Many of them will sign up just as fitness members which is a bit cheaper than being a tennis member — £120 as opposed to £290 just to join — and then it's £44 a month for tennis with free use of the courts as well as squash, badminton and the gym, whereas a health/fitness member will pay £34.50 a month. But it is the whole package that works and David Lloyd's name being synonymous with tennis only adds to the feeling that this is still very much a tennis club even though only one-third of the total membership are tennis members.'

Watt believes strongly that developing the club atmosphere with ladies' mornings and junior academies for tennis, and club nights with entertainment, sets David Lloyd Leisure apart from the ITI Centres which have sprung up under the LTA scheme and which are open to the public on a pay-as-you-play basis.

There is an allure about the game of tennis that survives changing mores and fashions and sporting tastes. Ever since Major Walter Wingfield patented a game which he called Sphairistike back in February 1874, because he thought it might resemble something played in ancient Greece, lawn tennis, as it was also known, has been an irresistible attraction to people of a certain social class who wished to consort with their fellows in a convivial sporting ambience. It became the sideshow attraction at the *thé dansants* held at the Carlton in Cannes during the roaring Twenties when Suzanne Lenglen was the toast of the Riviera. And a decade later Hollywood had adopted the sport with a vengeance as Gary Cooper, Marlene Dietrich, Charlie Chaplin and Errol Flynn were amongst the host of film stars to be found in their courtside boxes at the Los Angeles Tennis Club during the Pacific Southwest Championships. At this high celebrity level, stars as diverse as Peter Ustinov, Jean-Paul Belmondo, Cliff Richard and Seal are to be found at Wimbledon and tournaments all round the world, enhancing the profile of the sport by their presence. This filters down to the affluent middle class and it is there that the sport has become stuck — cast solidly in a mould of snobbism and elitism that has been incredibly difficult to shake off. Despite the fact that all manner of small tennis clubs in Britain and, indeed, all over the Continent, have been as basically affordable as their facilities were plain basic, the image has lingered of the faintly rich patting balls about behind the walled-off splendour of luxurious country clubs.

Even the proliferation of public park courts in America, where there are few more egalitarian sporting experiences to be found than playing alongside a Manhattan housewife in Central Park, has done little to alter the perception that tennis is not a game for the masses and certainly not for children of the deprived inner cities. Some of us, through programmes like the Gerulaitis Grassroots Foundation, have tried to get the message across that tennis can be a game for everyone but, believe me, it has been hard work, primarily because organisations like the LTA and USTA will not provide enough funds and dedicate enough time to taking the game into the 'difficult' areas.

So the social label still firmly affixed to the game's body politic has been a mixed blessing, heightening the image on the one hand while erecting needless barriers on the other. To some extent David Lloyd's success has helped to blur the social images because, although firmly middle class, the Leisure Centres have helped to broaden the base in the suburbs and create more places for people to play. And not just those who can afford £44 a month. At all DL Centres, the local council is offered a certain amount of time each week to bring in children of their choosing for coaching sessions or free play time. Some councils take up this offer, others squander the opportunity to get some dangerously bored and poorly directed kids off the streets and into a sport that could hold their attention and teach some self-discipline.

Renfrew District Council is one of the enlightened bodies that do opt to make use of the 250 hours a year available to local children, and neighbouring schools are offered time at fifty pence per pupil. Watt is very keen to involve the local youth and has taken a hard-line stand over the financial attractions of indoor soccer as a result.

'There is no doubt that there would be a huge demand for five-a-side soccer if I allowed it into the club,' he said. 'Scotland's soccer mad so there is every chance it would be even more successful than it has been at Heston. But it's not what I want to bring to the club. The type of membership it would attract along with the foul-mouthed language that seems to be part and parcel of five-a-side soccer, which is a very intense and highly competitive sport, is not what I want for our youngsters. In a relatively restricted indoor environment I don't want little kiddies doing their clinic just a few yards away being exposed to a lot of swearing. At Heston it is less of a problem because they have their soccer in an enclosed area. If I did it here it would be out the back, on a regular field, where we have four acres to play with. I could probably make a lot of money off that — but not at the expense of the family atmosphere we have been at pains to build up. We cater for all ages, all the way from Munchkin Classes for tennis which start at the age of four to veteran nights where some of the oldest players will be around seventy-five.'

The four-year-olds wielding a racket are not the youngest bairns to be found at David Lloyd Leisure Centres. As at most other clubs, Renfrew has a thriving and over-subscribed creche where mothers can leave little Johnnie for the day, or only for a matter of an hour or two, in the care of trained nurses. There is a capacity at this club of thirty toddlers for the day and another twenty-four to thirty for shorter periods, but Watt is intending to increase capacity in the near future because the demand is so great.

For adults, the facilities offer various ways to cool off after getting all hot and sweaty on a Stair Master. A spacious bar and restaurant is augmented by a conference room that is normally divided into three separate rooms named Boris Becker, John McEnroe and David Lloyd. Kim Matheson, daughter of Harry and Carole and sister to the big-serving pro Ross Matheson, is keeping the family tennis tradition alive by working at the club as Marketing Director in charge of all entertainment and functions. Kim arranges weddings and club meetings and special nights like the all-night party that survived the disappointment of Frank Bruno's demise at the lethal hands of Mike Tyson — a mismatch that did not start until about five in the morning, Glasgow time.

By then most people had had too much to drink which was no surprise to anyone, but Watt was still not prepared to accept the behaviour of one member who had used foul language and had abused a waitress.

'He's out,' said Watt. 'I'm not putting up with that kind of behaviour no matter what hour it is and no matter how much has been drunk. He's coming to see me in a wee while but it won't do any good. Once you allow that sort of thing to creep in the whole atmosphere we are trying to create goes down the drain.'

The right kind of atmosphere is created by the kind of evening Kim Matheson arranged as a fund-raiser for the families of the Dunblane massacre which raised £20,000. Kim is just one of a large core of bright young staff Watt has gathered about him including Blane Dodds, a former junior player, in sales and marketing and Gail Brown, a qualified accountant with a business degree from Robert Gordon's University in Aberdeen. Gail had never heard of David Lloyd Leisure when she saw an ad in the paper and decided to apply.

'The funny thing was my husband also applied!' she laughed. 'And I got it! Better still it didn't cause a divorce. It probably worked out for the best, too, because I think I probably have the better temperament for this kind of job which is very unlike anything you would find working in a normal accountancy firm.'

Gail obviously enjoyed the informality of finding a chairman of the board wandering in unannounced and winding her up over some perceived error in the salary cheques.

'David's great to work for because he's so keen and so involved,' she goes on cheerily. 'Everything from picking up dirty cups and paying for his own coffee to coming at you with info off the top of his head. You'd better know your stuff because he's hard but fair. I must say it still gives me a bit of a buzz to go home and say that I've been chatting with the chairman. Someone at my level wouldn't find themselves doing that at many companies.'

Insight V

Exhilaration

'I love driving fast and beautiful cars. I find it exhilarating to feel the speed and responsiveness of these magnificent pieces of machinery. Not that my first car was exactly magnificent, but it still lingers in the memory as one of the biggest thrills of my life — the purchase for exactly fifty pounds of a Ford Prefect. Second hand, of course. I was so happy that I promptly drove my mother all the way up to her parents' place in Newcastle. Somehow it got us there but it didn't get me back. Half-way home, it conked out and I had to leave it on a garbage dump.

'My first proper car was the Fiat 850 Sports that I drove all over Europe. It was a great car and stood up to all sorts of roads and tough handling. Now I seem to have graduated to Ferraris. Actually I have three of them. They are my indulgence. I have a saloon type Ferrari, a blue 456 which gets me about pretty well and then, for sportier occasions, I have an F355 Spider, a red one. It's a two-seater and has been described in the motoring press as the best car ever built. Then, in the garage because you really can't drive it anywhere, is a Formula One F50, just an amazing machine which I bought for £350,000. It's an investment — at least, that's what I tell my wife.

'As I've said, I don't enjoy flying and I'm not crazy about trains, so driving is one of my great pleasures. I can relax in my cars. I turn the stereo on and have a good time. Relaxing but always exhilarating, too.'

Chapter 14

Reading

The David Lloyd Leisure Club which sits by the Thames on the eastern edge of Reading, not far from the University, is surrounded by a couple of construction sites and a lot of unturned land. There is not a residence in sight. Promising. There was even less construction on it when Lloyd decided to accept Oracle's offer of a joint venture and David still thought it was promising. Which, for a man whose site-finding philosophy is based on 'location, location, location', takes a bit of explaining.

'In a couple of years, this will be one of the biggest business parks around London,' says Lloyd. 'Fifteen thousand people are going to be working here and when it's finished it will be spectacular. You've got the Thames and the boats right there, which is great in one way but a bit restricting, because the field in between us and the river bank is untouchable and already our members are asking for tennis courts. At the moment there is no way we can get the space to build any. But maybe we can work something out in the future.'

The Reading Club, which opened in June 1995 with 300 members, is primarily a fitness club with only a badminton court and a large 25-metre swimming pool, tented in the winter, to offer respite from the customarily daunting array of running, pushing and stretching machines which numbered eighty-five at the last count. That, however, has not hindered the inexorable membership growth, which in April 1996 stood at 1,400.

The club was built by Oracle, a multi-national company dealing in computer software, which began operations in the UK eleven years ago. Tim Caiger, Oracle's Director of Real Estate and Facilities, is in charge of the operation and was instrumental in setting up a search for some method of drawing people to the site long before the main infrastructure of a business park was up and running.

'We saw the attraction of the fitness and leisure industry and started looking around for the market leaders,' Caiger explained after he had dropped by the club for a lunch-time snack from his offices at the nearby building site. 'We had a look at various alternatives, including the people at Riverside who have a lovely club farther down the Thames near Richmond. But two things immediately impressed me about David Lloyd Leisure. Firstly the name was known, not just because of the success of the clubs already in existence, but because of David himself — here was a guy who had played at Wimbledon and people respond to that. Then there was his personal reaction to our enquiries. He said he'd come down and see us straightaway and you found yourself dealing with someone who knew his business inside out. He could quote you the price of brickwork out of the back of his head. And you were talking to the top man first hand. That is always a plus.'

The top man was back on site on this blustery April day, unannounced until he parked his blue Ferrari outside the front entrance from where Vivienne Scott, the club manager, could tell at a glance that the boss had arrived.

'No, I didn't know he was coming this time, although he often does give us warning,' she laughed. 'But I don't worry about that. It's good to have him around so that we can talk things over face to face. He has a very pleasant, informal approach to running the company and doesn't expect the red carpet.'

Lloyd and his young manager needed to discuss the problem of overcrowding in the locker room where there were not nearly enough showers for all the sweaty bodies using the machines.

'It's a design problem that we are going to have to take care of,' said Lloyd. 'We get a lot of complaints about it but, happily, people don't seem to leave. Maybe Vivienne is persuasive enough and makes them realise that we are aware of the problem and are genuinely trying to do something about it.'

Before Tim Caiger arrived, Lloyd had walked over to the bar, ordered a couple of coffees and immediately paid for them out of his own pocket. He'll never ask for anything at any of his clubs that he doesn't pay for himself. For that reason, and possibly for that reason alone, he is able to implement a policy which stipulates that all staff pay for their own lunches and whatever else they consume while on duty.

'It's true that we have a small amount of money added to our pay packets to make up for it, but it is not a popular rule,' admitted Vivienne Scott who has had experience working at other clubs, notably the upmarket establishment at Blackfriars. 'But we sort of get on with it because of the example David sets.'

Vivienne heads up a staff of sixteen at Reading, including cleaners who work through the night and the maintenance manager, Steve Cooke, who is in at six in the morning to make sure that the machines are working and the showers are not hanging off the wall.

'The cleaning of the club presents our biggest constant headache,' admitted Vivienne. 'We have seven hundred people moving through inadequate locker room facilities on a daily basis and the mess that creates is unbelievable.'

In line with the Lloyd philosophy of 'do it yourself if it's costing too much', DL Leisure recently bought into an established cleaning company, Ridgway. 'We were spending £800,000 a year on cleaning without seeing a cent in return,' he said. 'Now we spend the same amount but end up with a £100,000 profit.'

At Reading, however, expansion is urgently required if the increasing membership is to be properly catered for. No one is more aware of this than David Lloyd and he is asking for his members' indulgence.

'As usual there are all sorts of planning permits and council bureaucracy to overcome before we can get the place the way we want it,' he says. 'But unlike the experiences we have had elsewhere, these members are being pretty patient about it.'

That, as he says, is not always the case. If one thing has reared its ugly head time and again to impede the speed of David Lloyd's intended progress it has been the great British refusal to believe that something good is going to happen. He makes a promise, which he fully intends to keep, and people shout him down. 'Nah, you're just saying that — you're just like all the rest of them, promises, promises . . .'

The rest of whom? Have so many people been let down so often that they believe everyone is just a wide boy on the make? Judging from much of what Lloyd has witnessed this, sadly, seems to be the case.

When DL Leisure bought out the David Lanz fitness clubs in Bournemouth and Ringwood on the edge of the New Forest in 1994, the presentation meeting for members revived all the worst memories of the Beckenham Place Park fiasco. Two hundred people attended and a large percentage of them were hostile. Lloyd was shouted down when he insisted he would not be raising membership fees. Booing broke out. Then, finally, one middle-aged lady walked up to the stage, took the microphone out of David's hand and addressed the gathering. 'You have been nothing but rude to Mr Lloyd throughout these whole proceedings. The behaviour has been disgraceful.'

Some members had the decency to look sheepish, but the general mood remained one of total scepticism. The staff were suspicious as well, but Lanz helped by staying on to work under Lloyd and, after about a year, everyone was starting to realise that Lloyd had meant what he said. The fees had not gone up although the membership had — from 500 to 2,700 by April 1996 at Bournemouth, and from 1,000 to 1,324 at Ringwood where DL Leisure had built three indoor courts.

Lanz's staff took a little while to come round to the Lloyd way of doing things, too, but now they seem to appreciate the benefits of being part of a motivated team. The manager at Ringwood, Simon Phillips, cites working in an environment that is relaxed and stress-free as the most enjoyable aspect of working for David Lloyd, while the majority of managers seem to enjoy the unpredictable nature of the job. 'You never have two days the same,' says Chris Brooks at Enfield. 'It's always a challenge.'

It can also be amusing. At Eastbourne, Patrick Renn still chuckles at the memory of two very attractive young Swedish students assuming that the steam room was a ladies only area and marching in stark naked. In fact, the place was full of golden oldies, still male enough to suffer near cardiac arrest at the vision which appeared through the steam. At Ringwood it got a bit raunchier than that. A couple had to be asked to leave the jacuzzi because they had become a little bit too excited by the bubbles.

But in hearing from the managers, the satisfaction in working for a growing enterprise that many describe as the best of its kind in the country shines through. And the impact David Lloyd has on his staff is always apparent. Jane Hall, manager at the Eastbourne Ten-Pin Bowling Club, probably put it best. Asked why she enjoyed working for David, she said, 'Because he is a real person and not just a name, and I am a person and not just a number.'

Insight VI

Perception

'It always used to bug me that when we were doing an analysis presentation or giving new results and capitalising up to £100 million, which is not peanuts, we were still listed as small. I used to arrive at these places and look on the list and see "Small Companies — first on the left", and I'd say to the people running these things, "OK, you could say we're small but we're not that small, we're over £100 million. Just from a PR point of view why don't you re-name it?" It's perception. It's not necessarily what you are but what people think you are that counts in business. Even if we are small, I want people thinking big. Think small and you'll get small ideas. Be labelled small and people will bypass you with the best deals and offer them to the company with a higher profile even if, in reality, they are not much bigger than you are. You don't have to go over the top about it. Just don't downgrade yourself unnecessarily. It's PR and perception and it's half the battle.'

Chapter 15

Mixing Sport and Business

It was in a night club called Jacky O's just off the Via Veneto that John Newcombe and Charlie Pasarell resolved to quit talking and actually do something about the need for a players' association. The idea wasn't new and they were far from being the only players or officials who recognised the need for an organisation that, eighteen months later, was formed as the Association of Tennis Professionals, later to become known as the ATP Tour. But they became part of a group that actually got off their backsides and did something about it.

That conversation in Rome in 1971, between two young men famous for nothing other than their ability to wield a wooden tennis racket, would hardly have suggested the start of something big. Yet it was just one of several significant occurrences around that time which proved to be the sowing of the first seeds of a phenomenon that has now blossomed into an enormous industry — professional sport.

The industry which, only in the last few years, has started to make a serious impact on serious-minded people in the world's financial institutions now affects so many businesses and enterprises that I wonder how long it will take for those people who make up the application forms for credit cards and questionnaires concerning occupation to add it to those long lists of just about every other activity known to man. Only if the far-flung world of professional sport took six months off, and all those basketball teams, tennis players, footballers and golfers stopped playing and travelling, would hotels, airlines, travel companies, telecommunication firms, restaurants and banks feel the cold draught of a severely depleted bottom line.

In this respect I am speaking mainly of the performing side of professional sport, but entrepreneurs like David Lloyd have created businesses that are just as much part of the whole burgeoning industry. Sport, for better or for worse and certainly for richer rather than poorer, is huge business. And if anyone still looks down on the bulk of the participants as 'just dumb athletes', they will have a tough time explaining why so many have gone on to become quite so successful, either in or apart from the sport that gave them their first opportunities.

'Clearly sport and business do mix,' declared an article in the *Investors Chronicle* in April 1995. Pointing out that the two endeavours share a common lexicon, the publication went on to quote various sportsmen who had succeeded in the boardroom, amongst them England rugby coach Jack Rowell and former England and Middlesex spinner Phil Edmonds, who used to monopolise the dressing-room phone before the arrival of the mobile enabled him to wheel and deal with his pads on, desperately hoping that Mike Gatting would stay in long enough for him to agree a price.

Edmonds, who until recently was chairman of a property company he formed called Middlesex Holdings, said, 'Sometimes you walk into a business meeting knowing full well that the only reason they saw you was to talk about cricket. But the pros far outweigh the cons. Because I was a prominent cricketer, I was able to meet prominent businessmen.'

Rowell is very clear about the talents required to be successful in and outside the sporting arena. 'There is very little difference between running the England rugby team and turning round Golden Wonder Crisps,' said Rowell who was director of the food group Dalgety until 1994. 'The actual process of having goals and a strategy and implementing a business plan apply equally.'

Another rugby player who has discovered how to use muscle of a different kind off the field is David Perry, a towering presence in the England pack in the Sixties who captained the XV in 1964–65. Perry, who is chairman of the John Waddington games group, successfully fought off hostile takeover bids from Robert Maxwell during that period of the Eighties when the tycoon was riding roughshod through the country's financial institutions.

'If you're going to be a decent rugby player, you need a certain amount of controlled aggression,' Perry told *Investors Chronicle*. 'And I suppose some of that was helpful against Maxwell.'

If one was to make a world ranking list for successful business-men with tennis backgrounds, Jan Leschly would almost certainly come out No. 1. A former Danish Davis Cup star and Wimbledon quarter finalist, Leschly has had a meteoric career in the pharma-ceuticals industry and is now chief executive of SmithKline Beecham, Britain's second largest drugs company and, according to the *Financial Times*, was paid a salary of £1.8 million before bonus-es in 1995. Only the rugby player Tony O'Reilly, a British Lion and Ireland wing three quarter before becoming President of Heinz and a media tycoon, has outstripped him amongst those from any sport who have dealt with British business.

Leschly, with his outgoing personality and sharp mind, is one of the few to have carved out a highly successful career in a business totally unrelated to the game he played so well. Others who have put their knowledge of tennis and its related businesses to profitable use are legion. John Newcombe, literally making a trade mark out of his moustache, set up a Hong Kong-based clothing company which he eventually sold in the mid-Eighties for over a million dol-lars. Charlie Pasarell, who could never be accused of thinking small, took a couple of stabs at creating the tennis centre of his dreams — like getting a Japanese investor to help him buy four miles of the north Puerto Rican coast — before he and two partners secured a big enough loan to build the beautiful Grand Champions resort, complete with five star hotel and 10,500-seat tennis stadium, at Indian Wells in the Californian desert. He now runs the Chris Evert Cup and Newsweek Cup, back-to-back tournaments on the WTA and ATP Tours that constitute the biggest annual two-week sports extravaganza in California.

Pasarell was helped in his early business dealings by the man who envisaged it all, Donald Dell, a graduate of Yale, who told the US Davis Cup team he captained in the late Sixties, 'Stick by me and I'll make you all millionaires.' The team consisted of Pasarell, Arthur Ashe, Stan Smith, Bob Lutz and Marty Riessen. Dell was as good as his word. Firstly, with two partners Lee Fentress and Frank

Craighill and later under the name of ProServ, Dell founded a management company that, in the early days, was as influential as the International Management Group which had been created not long before by that other sporting visionary Mark McCormack.

Like his Yale contemporary Eugene Scott, who founded the widely respected magazine *Tennis Week* and has run such diverse events as the Masters at Madison Square Garden and the Kremlin Cup, a $1.1 million event on the ATP Tour in Moscow, Dell used his education and natural business acumen to shape the future of a sport that came bursting out of its amateur corsets in 1968 to grow fatter faster than even these progressive thinkers had ever imagined. In doing so, Dell was assisted throughout those early formative years of Open Tennis by Jack Kramer, one of the game's greatest promoters who had kept the professional game alive through his famous touring troupe led by Pancho Gonzales, Lew Hoad and Tony Trabert in the dark days of the Fifties and Sixties when anyone who earned a cent from the game was automatically banned from Wimbledon and all the other great traditional championships. Such was the publicity surrounding Kramer's controversial but invariably successful attempts to lure one Wimbledon champion after another to his stable, that many casual followers of the game forgot that Jack was a great player himself, having won Wimbledon in 1947 and played on his own tour until he retired from competition in 1954, frequently beating Gonzales in the process.

Kramer, who had failed to last past his freshman year at college, was amongst the first of many who had not enjoyed the benefit of an Ivy League schooling to make the move from baseline to boardroom with great agility. A Welshman, Mike Davies, one of the pros Kramer had signed for his tour, offered one of the best examples. Like Lloyd, Davies had not been a great student in Swansea and had little formal education after the age of fifteen. But he always knew how he wanted to see professional tennis develop and spent a while one evening during the old London Professional Championships at Wembley's Empire Pool telling me about it. That must have been around 1962. Six years later, Lamar Hunt, the sports nut amongst the oil-rich Hunt brothers from Texas, offered Davies the chance to put his ideas into practice. As boss of World Championship Tennis, the pro group Hunt formed just before tennis went Open, Davies suddenly found himself lunching with Dallas oilmen and cutting deals worth hundreds of thousands of dollars. It was a big leap for a former British No. 1 who had been used to arguing with the LTA over ten pounds six shillings and eightpence on his expenses. But, given budgets that would have made the boyos in the Welsh valleys fall down the mine shaft in shock, Davies learned fast and WCT, under his leadership, set the standard in the early Seventies with those unforgettable Rosewall-Laver finals in Dallas that the rest of the tennis world would try to emulate as it struggled to come to terms with the brave new world of professionalism. After thirteen years, Davies moved, less happily, into another high profile post as Executive Director of the Association of Tennis Professionals and then, completing an amazing circle of the game's power bases, returned to Baron's Court as Marketing Director for the International Tennis Federation.

By the time he retired last year and headed off into the wilds of the American Mid-west with his wife Trish in their mobile home, this less than perfectly educated Welshman had been raking in a salary plus bonuses with the ITF that, according to reports in *Tennis Week*, was verging on half a million pounds a year. Davies, with his alert mind and quick sense of humour, had learned on the hoof and was an expert in sports marketing, television production and dealing with the complex world of Japanese sponsor deals by the time he left Baron's Court.

Does the success of people like David Lloyd and Mike Davies suggest that one does not need a proper education to succeed? 'No, of course not,' says Lloyd. 'Life has changed since our day and competition for jobs is so much greater now. But I do think that some parents, quite understandably, tend to get very nervous about letting a talented child concentrate on their tennis at the expense of higher education. I get parents coming to me all the time seeking advice as to how they should juggle the twin demands of sport and education. I try to make them see the benefit of keeping their options open, and the only way to do that is to allow the youngster to go off and give tennis the priority during those vital years between seventeen and twenty. If you try it the other way round and pack them off to university, the chances of them succeeding if they start on the pro tour at twenty-one or twenty-two are very slim indeed. However you CAN go back to university at that age and do well. In fact, there are those who believe that many young people become far more receptive to teaching and classroom work after their teenage years and, in any case, they would have a far wider view of the world after three or four years on the tennis circuit, dealing with all the different languages and cultures, than they would had they arrived at university straight from school.'

Tim Henman, the first home-grown British tennis player to crack the world's top fifty since John Lloyd, is a prime example of what Lloyd is talking about and a very pertinent one, too, because David had a great deal to do with the development of Henman's career. When it came time to make a decision about the boy's future, Tim's father, a solicitor in Oxford, was very wary of putting tennis first.

'But Tim's parents listened to our advice about his potential and were very courageous in the end,' said Lloyd. 'It was obviously very worrying for them when Tim broke his ankle quite badly in Singapore when he was just starting to make progress in 1994. But since then he has justified everyone's faith in his ability and, financially, he will have no worries.'

This, of course, is the great difference between the opportunities that lie out there on the pro tour today compared with the late Sixties when Dennis Lloyd gave David a suitcase of dresses to sell to help him finance a trip to Africa. It can be a struggle if you never get out of the Satellite Circuits, but any player of real ability who can crack the top hundred soon finds himself making money no other youngster in their late teens or early twenties could dream about unless they happened to be a rock star. Henman earned £73,500 in prize money alone in 1995 and was set to triple that figure this year after his success at Wimbledon. Even those young whizz-kid dealers in the City's financial houses do not start earning that kind of money at the age of twenty-two.

And with Henman we are just talking about tennis. Although it might take them slightly longer to attain such earning power, Britain's golfers like Nick Faldo and Colin Montgomerie, and the Formula One racers such as Damon Hill and David Coulthard, become multi-millionaires as soon as they near the upper echelons of their sports. In a soccer-mad nation, Premiership footballers are collectively amongst the most affluent young men in the country, and now even rugby union stars are being signed to very healthy contracts by ambitious clubs like Richmond, Wasps and Saracens. It is all part of the growth of sport as a major profession, as far removed from the old amateur ethic of dirty whites, damp socks and dingy changing rooms on the edge of some God-forsaken field as one could imagine.

In his own sphere David Lloyd has done more than most to hasten the change, not just in facilities but also in attitude. Doomsayers who wrung their hands and bemoaned the state of British sport in general or tennis in particular never received much sympathy from the little Essex battler. When it became clear that the LTA was not producing an international player as good as or better than his brother, Lloyd decided it was time to do something about it. Once again he succeeded in a limited sort of way and might have done even better had the LTA not felt so threatened by the Slater scholarship scheme. It says much for Lloyd's more benevolent attitude towards the game's governing body that he seems to have accepted the scheme's closure with, by his standards, something approaching equanimity. But, before explaining how Jim Slater became involved in British tennis, it is necessary to put it in the context of Lloyd's well-aired views on how the game was being run in Britain.

Chapter 16

British Tennis

Having sat next to David Lloyd in a BBC Radio commentary box at Wimbledon for the better part of a decade, I am not unaware of what he has to say about the state of British tennis. Nor, more importantly, were the listeners. One of the first requirements of a good colour analyst on television or radio is that a) they know what they're talking about, and b) they have opinions and are not afraid to express them. Lloyd, in his distinctive Essex accent, filled the bill admirably even if, on occasion, his comment tended to be a little briefer than an out-of-breath commentator might have wished.

'Well, David, how do you see the match so far?'

'Boring.'

'Right . . . Sampras to serve, then, three all, second set.'

Lloyd didn't enjoy criticising the type of tennis served up on the fast green lawns of the All England Club, but he is one of those who firmly believe that the game has made grass an impossible surface on which to play because of the extra power of the rackets and the size of the modern player.

'The ball comes off a graphite racket 30 per cent faster than an old wooden one,' he points out. 'And the guys are serving from a height of about ten feet because so many of them stand about six and a half feet in their socks. Given those facts, it's no wonder you can't get the ball back. Grass is so fast when it's hard and dry and so slick when it's damp, that the matches are turned into a serving contest. You miss all the game's beauty and subtlety. There's nothing to watch.'

Thankfully Andre Agassi, proving he could return serve as well as Jimmy Connors, came along to offer some variety and ward off the worst of Lloyd's nightmares, but they were not his alone. John

Barrett would have loved to see a return to wooden rackets and John McEnroe would have been there to support him had it happened. But, of course, there was no chance. The International Tennis Federation's failure to determine what constituted a racket until well after thousands of graphite and steel Prince models with their startlingly large frames were selling in the shops, ensured that there would be no way of cracking down on the kind of trend cricket stamped on when Dennis Lillee appeared in Perth with his aluminium bat. For the club player that was a boon because it made a difficult game easier, but for the pros it simply fed the desire to skirt skill and replace it with raw power. As a result the game as a spectacle was diminished, most especially where it mattered most — at the world's premier tournament.

The All England Club has attempted to address the problem with softer balls and now balls that glow, but there is nothing much you can do about a fast grass court when someone like Goran Ivanisevic is serving on it.

Because he looks at the wider picture and cares passionately about how tennis is perceived, Lloyd wants Wimbledon to fly in the face of tradition and dig up the grass. For as long as John Curry remains chairman, that is not going to happen, although I have always felt that, if enough money was spent on perfecting the artificial grass and making it slower, the committee might see the advantage of installing a surface that not only played better but that would look far better on finals day than the present worn and scarred version of the beautiful Centre Court.

For the time being Lloyd is not expressing these views with as much vehemence because he has accepted the need to be a little more diplomatic now that he is Davis Cup captain. Considering how broad his criticism of the game in Britain had been, reaching far beyond the state of grass courts to the standard of coaching and the self-serving attitude of many people at the LTA, it took a great deal of courage on the part of the Management Committee to offer him the high profile role of the country's Davis Cup captain.

Given that it only required about four weeks a year of full-time commitment, there was never the slightest chance of Lloyd declining the offer. Patriotic to the core, he considered it, first of all, an honour but just as importantly he was excited by the idea of being able to make a first-hand contribution.

'I felt I could make a contribution because I was in a position that meant I didn't need a job; I was not seeking financial reward and therefore any comments I made would be based purely on what I believed to be right. I wanted to make a contribution and put something back into the game because I love it. I was prepared to put my head on the block. Criticising from the sidelines all the time gets very frustrating. I felt I had something to offer providing I was able to do it my way.'

Doing it his way meant that he reported solely to a Board of Directors at the LTA and that all team decisions such as choosing players, coaches and training conditions were his alone. With Billy Knight, whose wholehearted attitude to tennis endeared him to Lloyd, ready to retire after a brief time in charge following Tony Pickard's departure, David felt the moment was right and that a change in leadership would be good if for no other reason than a change shakes things up and produces results.

'Look at Crystal Palace this year,' Lloyd pointed out. 'They were terrible for most of the season until Dave Bassett took over and, with the same players, they ended up in the promotion play-offs. And then they lost to Leicester whose fortunes had also been turned inside out with the arrival of Martin O'Neill. Sometimes a change is good just because it is a change.'

Inevitably, Lloyd's criticism of the LTA has become muted since he took over as Davis Cup captain, but he is not reticent about what he believes should have been done in the past and where the problems lay. Coaching would probably have come top of his list, not merely the general standard of coaching in Britain but the way the coaches were deployed and the LTA's refusal until quite recently to import talent from abroad.

'There is no doubt that coaching levels in this country have been very poor,' says Lloyd. 'One of the main problems in my view was the decision by the LTA to consolidate all the talent at a central point like Bisham Abbey. That's all very well if you have some talent coming through, but a lot of the coaches out in the regions have not been good enough to develop what talent there was. It's like a wheel. If the outside of your wheel is weak, your centre can never be strong. Now that they have hired some good coaches like Ian Barclay and Peter Fleming, it is essential that you have some worthwhile talent coming through from the regions otherwise they have nothing to work with.'

If anyone doubts that Lloyd is correct in this analysis, they need only study the success of Swedish tennis over the past two decades. An amazingly high percentage of players from the Mats Wilander-Stefan Edberg generation came from small towns where an athletically minded young person's options were limited. Football was one possibility and tennis was very definitely another.

'As a kid I used to get on my bike and cycle through the snow to our local indoor tennis centre where there was always a good coach,' says Edberg who grew up in Vastervik. 'None of us were ever very far from somewhere to play and have lessons.'

Lloyd's fear is that British talent is being allowed to slip through the net or drift off into other sports. Some, like Sarah Loosemore, whose brother David was a member of Lloyd's Slater scholarship scheme, become so turned off by the whole system that they simply walk away.

'I just wonder what would happen if a potential Boris Becker emerged in Cumbria,' muses Lloyd. 'Would the LTA coach in, say, Carlisle be equipped to handle that kind of talent? Or would Carlisle United grab him and turn him into a centre half? I feel very strongly that it is absolutely essential to put your best people out in the field. Pay them more, elevate their status but have them developing the talent as it appears on their doorstep. Then maybe you don't even need a centre.'

It's radical thinking like this which sends cold chills of fear through the corridors at Baron's Court. No one is in any doubt as to the level of commitment Lloyd would demand if he ever got the top job, the one that has been held throughout the past decade by the former Slazenger boss Ian Peacock. The two of them had a talk recently and Peacock admitted that he had taken a step-by-step approach to rectifying the ills that afflicted the British game after the unproductive years of Paul Hutchins's leadership and that he realised Lloyd would probably have done it differently.

'Ian was right,' says David. 'We are different people. We'll never know which one of us would have been right because Ian has done it his way and has some good things to show for it. But I would have wanted people with a fanatical desire to make tennis the best sport in Britain and who were prepared to work long hours to achieve that. To get things done in the kind of situation that existed at the LTA in the Eighties you needed someone who was prepared to be a bit of a dictator; someone who wasn't afraid of making enemies. If you have the courage to do that you finally end up making a lot of friends because things start to improve. But, in the beginning, you have to bite the bullet and it can be painful.'

Lloyd has never hidden the fact that, in his areas of expertise, he wants things done his way. The staff at Heston were left in no doubt about that, nor were David's doubles partners. Sue Barker is probably much better equipped to handle some of the egos she runs into in television as a result of having played mixed doubles with the eldest Lloyd.

'When we first decided to play together, David was quite explicit,' Sue told me during a visit to Roland Garros during this year's French Open. 'He said, "I want you to serve and to return. Then just get out of the way and leave the rest to me and remember, anything that goes up in the air is mine!" That suited me perfectly. We got on well and had a bit of success, too, getting as far as the quarters at Wimbledon.'

Lloyd, of course, put as much into his mixed doubles as he did into any other endeavour. A tennis match was something to be won and Sue found him an exhilarating partner. There was mutual respect there, too, because Barker had done something very difficult for a British tennis player — she had won the French Open on that red clay over in Paris, backing up a magnificent forehand with a determination just about as gritty as the court beneath her feet. Why, Lloyd wondered, was she almost one of a kind? Why, every time he passed through the lounge at the Queen's Club, were there so many British juniors, both boys and girls, lolling around watching television?

Finally, after a few attempts on his own at bringing young players through to a higher level, Lloyd linked up with the financier Jim

Slater who, like Charles Haswell, was another LTA reject. Slater had already enjoyed some success with chess, a game he was familiar with inasmuch as he had sent young British chess players to Russia to study and play with the grand masters. Although not a tennis player himself, Slater used to go to Wimbledon every year and soon became impatient with the lack of home-grown players to grace the world's greatest championship. So he approached the LTA but did not receive the kind of enthusiastic response to his proposals that he was hoping for. So, just like Haswell, he turned to David Lloyd.

'We quickly discovered we were after the same thing,' said Lloyd. 'We wanted to give talented kids the opportunity to pursue tennis all year round while still getting a proper education. He asked me what I thought was wrong and I told him that, firstly, we weren't getting players with sufficient athletic ability and, secondly, we were getting them too late. I felt sure that we needed to get the kids at ten and eleven instead of fourteen, which was what the LTA maintained. I think I've been proved right on that one — fourteen is too late and the LTA have virtually conceded the point now. We also needed to cast the net wider and get kids who were athletic as well as being ball minded, because it's no use having lovely strokes if you can't run fast enough to get to the ball. So we formed the Slater Scheme and then ran ads in the *Daily Mail* to invite kids to come and be tested. I asked Frank Dick, Great Britain's athletics coach at the time, to help out, and after we'd put them through some tests with a racket, Frank basically ran them this way and that until they dropped. And it was the ones who kept going that we were after. Obviously some were just fitter than others, which is something that can be rectified, but you have to look for something else; you have to try and spot the ones who are simply giving up, who are kidding you and maybe even kidding themselves, that they are at the end of their tether. Often it's difficult to spot and sometimes you make mistakes, but I sort of developed a sixth sense about it and we ended up being more right than wrong.'

One of the boys chosen to attend Reed's School, which was within easy driving distance of Raynes Park where they would get three hours' coaching a day, was Mark Moreso. Don't bother looking for him alongside Tim Henman at next year's Wimbledon. He won't be there.

'Mark ended up coaching for a time and then I think he went into the City as a trader,' said Lloyd. 'He'd be good at that because he had a very sharp mind but he never made it on a tennis court because I didn't think he was a competitor, which was really sad because this boy had more talent than I have ever seen in a tennis player. He was a left-hander and, at the age of eleven, he could do anything with a tennis ball. I thought I'd found a Wimbledon champion. I thought, "this kid's going to be the next Rod Laver." He was our first kid and he stayed until he was about fifteen and people were astonished when he didn't make it. Peter Fleming came down to see him and told me not to worry because John McEnroe had been a bit like him at sixteen, bags of talent but not winning much, but, in my view, Mark just didn't have what it takes to guts it out.'

Apart from Morenso, Henman and David Loosemore were the first boys to sign up for the Slater Scheme and soon started to benefit from the regular school curriculum and the daily coaching sessions at Raynes Park that began at three o'clock every afternoon except Sundays.

'Soon we took more boys on because it was all working so well,' says Lloyd. 'We had a headmaster in David Prince who was dedicated to the idea, and it was obvious the boys were getting the most out of it. And they should have done because I had Onny Parun, Donald Watt and my brother Tony going with them one-on-one most days, which is something else I believe in. If you have a special talent, it needs special attention and these were top-class coaches giving one pupil their full attention. And it worked because after a year, we won every Under-14 title for boys in the country. The LTA couldn't ignore that sort of impact and I think they started to change their thinking as a result.'

One boy who had to wait a little for his taste of success was Tim Henman. Within a matter of weeks of joining the scheme, the solicitor's son from Oxford started to suffer from the kind of growing bone disease that affects farm boys who bail too much hay at a young age. Basically it means that you have been swinging your arms about too much and putting too much stress on a growing body. Tim was distraught and fearful that he would have to leave

Reed's, but Lloyd insisted on sticking with him even though he never hit a ball for nine months.

'And when I did start again, I was able to hit literally for one minute at a time to start with,' Henman admitted. 'It was a slow, painful business but David supported me and I'll always be grateful for that.'

Lloyd supported all the boys right up to that fateful moment when he had to take a long cold look at someone and ask himself the only question that mattered — 'Is he going to make it?' The answer would be vital to the boy's future because the whole basis of the Slater Scheme was that sport should take its place alongside education up to the age of sixteen and then actually supersede it. Lloyd was telling parents to allow their sons to put their tennis first because he was convinced they would make world-class players which, in his book, meant attaining a ranking of fifty or sixty on the ATP computer. But if he felt they would fall short of that, there was only one honest thing to do.

'I had to tell the parents and the kids at fourteen and fifteen, "Look, you're going to be good, but you can't be world class. That's my opinion." And I had many rows with parents who said, "Of course he will," and I said, "I'm just telling you my opinion. If you don't believe it, that's fine. I will pay for his education up to sixteen, but his education should now be put first and his tennis second." That was the job I had to do. And I think the LTA should do exactly the same. You cannot and should not carry people who won't make it because, in fact, all you're doing is actually ruining their lives. You're not giving them anything else but a free trip around the world. Fine. But when they come back, what do they do? And if they're bright, they should go to university if they can't make it in tennis. There are too many kids going around the world who cannot and never will make a living out of this game. You might feel it's unfair. But it's a fact of life. You can't push someone to be someone he's not going to be. Most importantly it's unfair on him. I had an obligation to give them an out before it was too late. But I had parents who didn't like me for it.'

The parents of a boy called Adrian Blackman were amongst those who did not welcome the news but, once they had accepted that Lloyd had the best interests of their son at heart, they allowed David to encourage Adrian to get a place at Stirling University after he had passed his A levels and he went on to captain the tennis team.

'And that's the way it should be for those who fall just short of what I feel is necessary to make it in the big time. It's no disgrace and, after a few tearful moments, his parents realised that I had no axe to grind, I was just doing what I thought to be best. He'll go on to get a good degree and, hopefully, a good job. He's followed a path that is best for him while Henman, who had that little bit extra, has proved he has what it takes after cracking the top forty this year.'

Not all Lloyd's choices for stardom have been as successful. Jamie Delgado certainly looked like the real thing when he became the first British player to win the Under-14 title at the Orange Bowl, the world's premier junior championship which is held in Miami at Christmas every year. But, hampered by lack of height, Delgado has struggled since, although he is still battling on in the Challengers and on the Satellite Circuits, testing-grounds that eventually sort out the nearly men from those who possess all the varied ingredients required to make a champion. There is still every hope that Delgado will make an impact at a higher level.

James Baily was a stranger case. This powerfully built lad from Hampshire surprised everybody by winning the Boy's Under-18 title at the Australian Open in Melbourne in 1994, only to quit the game less than a year later. Didn't like it, couldn't take it — who knows? It is a syndrome that has affected various other British players of promise who have a sip at the well of opportunity and decide they don't like the taste. It may be they are saner than the rest, for the life of a nomad, a lone warrior competing against the world, friend and foe alike, is not for everyone.

At any rate, the Slater Scheme proved that, with proper coaching and the required attention to detail, a system could be set up whereby Britain could discover players who could play. However, difficulties with the LTA made it impossible for Lloyd and Slater to continue.

David Lloyd shakes his head in despair. 'I don't know, I really don't. I've seen too much now to get as upset at that sort of thing as

I used to, but the LTA know what I think. We have a good relationship now and Richard Lewis is a nice guy who is trying to do a good job. But being afraid of competition is not the way to achieve anything. If I had my way, all the best coaches in Britain would be encouraged to set up their own schemes, funded initially by the LTA and, after two years, the best ones would survive. It would be tough but that's competition. I would be in there fighting and I am sure Chris Bradnam, Alan Jones and others would be, too. And it wouldn't half save the LTA a bit of money. Because it would cut out your centre core of costs. That is what's ruining so many businesses — the cost of their centralised bureaucracy that spends its life telling the managers on the ground, the people out in the regions, what sort of beer they should put in the bar. I don't know if Boddington's sells in Glasgow, and I'm not about to tell Donald Watt to order it. That's his decision and he shouldn't have to report up ten thousand layers to get it approved. It's called flat management and that's the way we're moving now, allowing the managers to be in charge of the decision-making for their areas of expertise.'

Radical surgery on coaching squads is not the only thing Lloyd would change if he was ever to head the LTA. Clubs that had any policy restricting the use of courts by juniors would find themselves shivering outside the front door at Baron's Court pleading for their funding and their Wimbledon ticket allocation to be returned to them. But, until they changed, they wouldn't get so much as the time of day from Mr Lloyd.

'I would have any club that had ANY kind of policy restricting the juniors taken off the LTA registry IMMEDIATELY. And no Wimbledon tickets. Nothing burns me up more than to go to some of these places and see notices posted saying "No juniors on Saturday morning" or whatever. That just simply cannot be allowed to happen. No wonder we never produce any players. The LTA could put that into effect tomorrow if they wanted, and if I was in charge I would do it tomorrow.'

Playing-in tests, which is a policy at many clubs to screen new members, is something else that draws Lloyd's fire. And he doesn't care who knows it — even if it involves his own club and his own father.

'There was a hell of a row about eighteen months ago when my own club, the Westcliff Hardcourts, a good club with a high standard of player, suddenly decided to institute playing-in tests for new members. The argument started over whether these tests should be conducted by my father or the committee. So I told them I was coming down to attend the special meeting they had set up and everyone thought it was because I was going to make a big case for my father doing it. But when I got up to speak all I said was that I didn't think they should have playing-in tests in the first place. I mean, how are you ever going to pass a playing-in test if you can't play? And how are you ever going to start if your nearest club bars you before you have a chance to learn? The whole thing is absurd. Even people who can play a bit freeze under the pressure of a test. I just didn't understand why they would want to do it and I still don't. Members who can't play and who are keen to learn are precisely what a coach attached to a club wants. It keeps him busy. But the whole notion of frightening people away is one of the reasons why fewer people are playing. It's ruining the game.'

Chapter 17

Newcastle and the Davis Cup Captaincy

David Lloyd thought long and hard before recommending that the Euro/African Group II Davis Cup tie against Slovenia, that was due to be played at home in May 1996, be held at the Castle Farm Club in Gosforth.

'I hesitated because we had just bought the place,' Lloyd said. 'I knew there would be people who saw it as a self-serving move, but it just so happened that it suited our needs perfectly. There was no point in playing a tie against unknown opposition in London, and I wanted to make absolutely sure of victory by giving Greg Rusedski the fastest possible indoor court. So, in the end, I just decided to do what was right.'

In the end there were very few murmurs of disapproval. Located just a few miles outside Newcastle, Castle Farm was in the last throes of re-modelling when the tie was held, having been converted from its previous existence as an Indoor Tennis Initiative (ITI) Centre, and it proved an ideal venue which was well supported in a modest way by the local community.

'This was one example of an ITI Centre not being able to make it financially,' Lloyd explains. 'They were having problems paying back the loans and couldn't make enough profit to expand. So the LTA agreed to drop it as an ITI and pay back various loans. We came in and replaced one court with a gym and spent £1.5 million on various improvements, including a 25-metre pool. We upgraded the locker rooms, provided a better standard of food and generally tried to create the kind of club atmosphere that ITI Centres lack. Generally I think they do a great job in offering more opportunities to play, but the financial aspect has to be looked at again. It costs £13 an hour to play tennis in peak periods at an ITI, whereas our members at Castle Farm can now play as much as they want for £16 a month. That's 50p a day.'

Most members seemed quite content to forgo the pleasures of trying to improve their forehands for the weekend when David Lloyd brought his team to Newcastle, although I am sure there were a minority who grumbled. Club members can be notoriously unimpressed by having superior world-class players muscle in on their facilities no matter how important the occasion. Before the US Open was moved to Flushing Meadow, the crotchety old members, playing cards in the upstairs locker room at the West Side Tennis Club — better known as Forest Hills — were frequently abusive to the pros who crowded their space, behaviour that did not go down very well with such polite gentlemen as Stan Smith, Rod Laver and Manolo Santana. But, in the somewhat more modest surroundings of Castle Farm, everyone seemed genuinely pleased to see Britain's Davis Cup team, headed by Greg Rusedski, the world's fastest server, add a little lustre to their courts, even if the tie was being played at an embarrassingly low level for the Davis Cup.

Apart from having David's long-time friend Ralph Broomby on the committee, it was a bit of a family homecoming for the Lloyds. David's mother is from the North-East and Doris was soon surrounded by relatives in the lounge between matches. It was homely and fun, and even the press didn't mind being housed in the squash courts. But it turned out to be an interesting test for Lloyd's style of Davis Cup captaincy, because Tim Henman had to withdraw with a virus he had picked up in the Far East and the Slovenes turned out to be rather better tennis players than their dismal world rankings suggested. So much so, in fact, that Borut Urh, ranked 466, beat Mark Petchey on the opening day and with Mark still unable to shed his Davis Cup nerves, it was left to Greg Rusedski to ensure that he did not have to play a fifth and deciding rubber. Rusedski did so with a devastating display of power tennis against Urh, and Lloyd was able to relax.

'As captain, it is so important to get to know how your players react in stressful matchplay situations,' said Lloyd. 'You only learn by being with them out there on court and I am still searching for the key as far as Mark Petchey is concerned. He gets very uptight when things start to go wrong, and I have to find a way of easing the tension for him. Every player is different. With some it is better just to murmur encouragement; others feed off tactical hints and some prefer the rah-rah-rah type of approach. The best situations are like the one Greg created today, with a performance so focused and dominating that you don't have to say a word. Then the job becomes easy!'

Chapter 18

Whitbread

Before we examine the reasons for the crisis that erupted in the spring of 1996, a crisis that found David Lloyd one step away from walking out on his dream child and leaving Whitbread with an unruly, adopted offspring that was not at all potty-trained in the manner to which they were accustomed, it is necessary to discover why they established a relationship in the first place.

A conviction that the burgeoning leisure industry was ripe territory for his company's expansion plans, allied to a personal involvement in professional tennis during his days as Marketing Director, led Peter Jarvis, now Managing Director of Whitbread plc, to approach David Lloyd Leisure with a view to acquiring the fourteen clubs that existed in 1995. In doing so, he was under no illusions about the nature of the beast he was trying to snare.

For a start, Jarvis had done his homework. He had come to understand that it was the personality of their founder that drove the clubs and the man's business acumen that had made them profitable. But Jarvis also knew enough about David through his own contacts with tennis. During his days as Marketing Director of Whitbread, he had set in motion the highly successful partnership between Stella Artois, one of the Whitbread beers, and the Queen's Club. It had started, as Jarvis recalls, when Frank Lowe of Lowe, Howard, Spink persuaded him to invest a quarter of a million pounds to advertise one of their lesser-known beers to sponsor a tennis tournament.

'Frank was certainly the motivating force behind the whole rejuvenation of the Queen's Club event,' says Jarvis. 'I had my doubts at first, especially when it rained for the first two days. I remember my wife was giving tea parties in the real tennis courts with water dripping on her. Then the weather changed and a young man called John McEnroe walked out into the sunshine and we never looked back. McEnroe was runner-up that year to Tony Roche and played the tournament for the next six years, winning it four times. He made the tournament.'

The substantial sponsorship deal, which has grown as the tournament has prospered over the years, effectively saved the London Grasscourt Championships, as they have been known historically, from extinction. As it was, they had ceased to exist between 1974 and 1976, having fallen victim to the savage political in-fighting that afflicted the professional game throughout the Seventies. Jarvis had listened to the LTA's arguments that Wimbledon desperately needed a proper grass court tournament to act as a lead-in to the Championships and, despite its state of faded grandeur, the nine-teenth-century Queen's Club would continue to be the obvious venue. Before the hiatus, the tournament had been held in front of the imposing Victorian clubhouse ever since 1890, when H. S. Barlow became the first of many famous names to raise the huge silver cup that Boris Becker won for the fourth time in 1996. Everybody from Anthony Wilding, Bill Tilden and Fred Perry to Lew Hoad and John McEnroe had played and won on the velvet grass courts that have always maintained their reputation for being amongst the very best in the world. All that was needed, Jarvis felt, was a heavy dose of modern marketing and the sponsorship money that went with it. The collaboration, to put it mildly, has been a success.

It is strange that Jarvis should lead his company towards the David Lloyd clubs because both, in totally separate ways, have had an enormous impact on the legendary Queen's Club which has always been the hub of tennis activity in Britain. Between them, directly and indirectly, they have played their part in helping Queen's give itself a facelift. Whitbread helped first by pouring money into the tournament, an event that suddenly became one of the most easily recognisable sporting occasions of the London season — a result of the unforgettable billboards Jarvis ordered to be plastered all over London. These portrayed John McEnroe, with the trademark headband of his early years, and Ilie Nastase, with a racket between his teeth, snarling at each other nose to nose. It was fabulous advertising and, with Jimmy Connors included in subsequent years, it merely served to heighten the sense of excitement and occasion that tennis generated in the early Eighties. The crowds came pouring back into Queen's and, with box holders given straw boaters with the red ribbon, a certain style was reintroduced that was both financially rewarding and socially uplifting. The caché of the event began to rub off on the club and the cash reserves improved. But renovation was still slow in coming, and it was not until Heston opened and scores of disgruntled members sped down the motorway in search of clean, well-appointed indoor facilities that Clive Bernstein and his colleagues on the club committee heard the wake-up call. Four more indoor courts were added, and in recent years the improvements have been so startling that one has become almost nostalgic for the old Queen's Club lunches in the cafeteria-style restaurant at the back of the clubhouse where the movers and shakers of the tennis world would congregate through various decades — Derek Hardwick, Stanley Hawkins, David Gray, Ted Tinling, Mike Davies and whole generations of British players who would have been better off out on the circuit. The gossip was always better than the food and a lot livelier than the service, but it was homely if nothing else, and today's recently opened lounge with marble service counters and potted palms gives Queen's a completely different feel.

'They've done a lot, no question about it,' says Lloyd, 'but we forced them to do something because they'd never had any competition before. In the end, we were the best thing that happened to Queen's.'

So, in a sense, Jarvis helped produce the funds and Lloyd provided the incentive for what has become a rejuvenation of one of the world's most famous tennis clubs. The members must love it.

It was inevitable that, sooner or later, Jarvis and Lloyd would run into each other and, indeed, some Whitbread executives soon found themselves on the same golf course as David whom they had been hearing about from Mike Gearing of James Capel, a golfing friend of David's who had been extolling the virtues of contemplating a takeover from the right kind of parent company. So he was a known quantity when Whitbread went looking for a leisure group to buy in 1995. And a very interesting one at that.

'We quickly discovered that David Lloyd Leisure was head and shoulders above the rest of the field both in reputation and as far as the physical premises were concerned,' said Jarvis. 'We knew what we wanted because we had been investigating this growing phenomenon of the leisure-style club in the States and Europe and, for a lot of reasons, we were satisfied that the David Lloyd Clubs were what we were after.'

The question that needs to be answered first is: why was a brewery interested in leisure clubs? To the public at large, if not to City analysts, the name Whitbread is still synonymous with beer. The pale brown bitter has been brewed by the Whitbread company for 230 years, long before the French Revolution, let alone any late twentieth-century revolution in living styles — a revolution that has been quickening in pace throughout the Nineties as people in Britain have followed their American cousins in becoming more health conscious.

Partly as a result of this, and partly because of changes in the taste of those of us who like a drink at the local, beer consumption was not merely static but, across the board, was in decline. So diverse are the company's interests now, that the brewery business is responsible for only 15 per cent of its overall profit. Out of 75,000 employees, only 5,000 work in beer. And if David Lloyd Leisure continues to grow at its present rate, that percentage will only get smaller. Despite the fact that Whitbread's marketing ability had kept brands such as Heineken, Boddington's Ale, Murphy's Stout and Stella Artois buoyant, it became obvious that hops were not going to hack it as far as future growth was concerned. So the company began looking for related businesses and either created or bought up such food chains as Beefeaters, Pizza Hut and the American hamburger chain TGI Friday's which had begun life as a singles bar on Third Avenue in Manhattan — a hang-out designed for the New York swingers of the Sixties who used the expression Thank God It's Friday.

Retail stores were next on Whitbread's list, hence the proliferation of Wine Rack and Bottoms Up, and then it was time to look at hotels.

'By the mid-Eighties we were ready to get into branded budget hotels of the type that take up 15 per cent of the market in France,' Jarvis explained. 'Then came the four-star hotels and finally we moved into Country Club hotels, all of which have golf courses attached and are now spread all over the country at places like Chepstow, Goodwood and the Forest of Arden.'

It was soon noted that not only did the golf members enjoy spending time in the bar, but also made full use of the swimming pool. Even more than the hotel guests, an important part of the Country Club hotels' business came from local membership. The regulars quickly created a club atmosphere and began demanding a wider range of facilities. But then the recession hit at the beginning of the Nineties and Whitbread, like so many other companies in similar fields, held its breath.

'But our fears never materialised,' said Jarvis. 'We had felt sure that, as people tightened their purse strings, their leisure activities would take the first hit. Exactly the opposite happened. The clubs had become such an important part of their social life that they cut back elsewhere and still went for their round of golf and drink in the bar.'

David Lloyd was experiencing precisely the same phenomenon and it was crucial to the growth he was able to maintain throughout the recession. 'People just stopped going abroad for their holidays and spent more time at our clubs,' Lloyd said, barely able to suppress a chuckle of contentment. 'It was amazing! There we were, bracing ourselves for the worst, and they kept on coming. Compared to a great many businesses we breezed through the recession.'

There are other examples of how dominant a part sport plays in people's lives. I remember asking John Gaustad, the proprietor of Sports Pages bookshop in the Charing Cross Road, if he was being as badly hit as the big chain bookstores down the street during the worst of the recession. 'Not at all,' he said. 'I have been pleasantly surprised by the lack of downturn in our business. Our customers are committed sports fans and apparently are willing to give up other things before they forgo the pleasure of the latest cricket annual or soccer biography.'

The way in which people were spending their money during the difficult years was as clear as night and day — literally — to Whitbread. 'The hotels continued to do great business with the local members but the bedrooms were going unused. If they had just been normal hotels it would have been a disaster.'

So the decision was taken to approach David Lloyd with a takeover offer and Jarvis knew up front that the bid would succeed or fail with the man himself. 'David was totally involved in the day-to-day running of his clubs,' Jarvis pointed out. 'He WAS the business. But we knew that we had to achieve the approval of David Lloyd himself if the bid was to be successful. He had to agree to place his shares in our hands.'

Before the public row erupted, coincidentally just prior to the Stella Artois Championships of 1996, Jarvis had insisted in our initial conversation that he was well aware that Lloyd was not your ordinary corporate figure. In fact he wasn't corporate at all and had never been slow in informing people of the fact. 'I think it's fair to say that David is not a big admirer of plc's,' said Jarvis. 'In the end we had to convince him that our style of doing business was as compatible with his as any two such entities could be.'

Lloyd was convinced — for a time. It was only four or five months later that he realised the ground rules were not working in the manner he had anticipated. The two men, hugely successful in their different fields, had thought they knew each other better than they did. The time eventually arrived — with painful inevitability to some of the more objective observers — when a major revision of thinking, perspective and operation would be required. But, initially, Lloyd was seduced by the fact that Whitbread had the reputation of being a friendly, well-run and enormously successful company with interesting ideas. Although he was not desperate to sell, no one needed to spell out to him the obvious benefits of becoming part of a far bigger entity which would be able to fund his own expansion plans far faster than he could. So he agreed to listen to Whitbread's offer which began at £180 million for thirteen David Lloyd Leisure Centres. When it was made clear that Whitbread wanted David Lloyd to stay on as Chairman AND Chief Executive Officer (the dual role would later become a contentious issue), everyone went back to the bargaining table and the final figure became £201 million, which many City analysts felt was too much. It is doubtful if they do now.

The budget projection Whitbread made when they took control of the clubs late in 1995 was a 25 per cent increase in business in the first six months — a tall order by any standards. Yet by May 1996, when the first six-month figures were released, David Lloyd Leisure was bang on track. To the end of Whitbread's financial year in February, sales had racked up £19.1 million with a profit of £5.1 million. That represented a turnover increase of 36 per cent, which was equivalent to the anticipated 25 per cent profit growth.

These figures were released less than a month before the lid blew off the kettle. There was no steam coming out of Jarvis's ears when he first spoke to me immediately after the excellent first half-yearly report. In fact he sounded extremely upbeat, as well he might.

'The trading performance is almost exactly equivalent to the expected growth, and that means that we will be able to accelerate the opening of new clubs, some of which are only being held back now because of planning permission problems,' said Jarvis. 'And we've achieved that by leaving them alone. David Lloyd's clubs exist today precisely as they were when we bought them. They maintain a separate identity within the parent company. This is in marked contrast to what is happening to the group of Marriott hotels that we bought about the same time. They are being absorbed into Whitbread in an operation that is structurally very different.'

It was that assertion of total independence that Lloyd found himself refuting so vigorously just a few weeks later. In the light of what transpired, it is interesting to note precisely what Jarvis told me during our first conversation. He made it clear on the one hand that he wanted Lloyd to stay on as head of DL Leisure, but spoke, too, of the fact that a man with such a fertile mind and restless energy would surely not be content to hang around after the task he had set out to achieve had basically been accomplished. He seemed, in fact, to be preparing the way for David's imminent departure.

'Frankly, I don't expect David to stay in his current position for another ten years,' Jarvis had said. 'Whatever the legal niceties of our relationship, I am sure we could come to some amicable agreement if he wanted to move on. I feel very strongly about the need for people to enjoy themselves while working for Whitbread and it has never been my policy to force anyone to stay just because a contract says so. I would hate to lose David because I have the utmost admiration for the way he runs his business. He knows everything there is to know about the business he has built up and you have to admire that expertise. In fact, the need for us to understand that expertise was one of the prime factors in our wanting to take over his company. We were buying his expertise if you like and, although we ended up paying £4 a share, time will show that it was a good price.'

At the time of this conversation early in April 1996, there was much speculation as to the possibility of Lloyd taking the next logical step in his rapprochement with the LTA and succeeding Ian Peacock as Managing Director. If appointing David as Davis Cup captain was a brave move on the part of an organisation that had been pilloried by him over the years, allowing him free rein to run the entire organisation would really have taken some nerve. But, as Jarvis was the first to admit, no one else was remotely as qualified on all fronts to take charge of British tennis and give it the kick up the backside that was needed to project it into the twenty-first century. An ex-player and a proven business wizard who knows everyone in tennis and is known and admired throughout the British business world? Those are tough credentials to match and if the LTA were to shy away from offering him the job they would need to produce something akin to Superman with a great backhand and a computer's brain for figures before anyone would accept they had made the right choice. However, there were signs in the spring that the LTA Committee of Management were desperately searching for ways to avoid grasping such a bristly nettle. At considerable cost, they were intending to call in a head-hunting firm to sift through all the applications and then recommend to them a short-list of three or four, after interviewing the leading candidates. And what, one wonders, would they discover that we don't already know? That Jan Leschly of SmithKline Beecham is available? Hardly likely, and as Leschly is the only man working in Britain with equivalent credentials — business wizard and former international tennis player — the whole exercise seems pointless. John Barrett and John Beddington, who gave up seventeen years at the helm of Canadian tennis to join the new British-based management company Masters International in 1995, were considered to be the only viable alternatives to Lloyd by most people inside the game — but outside Baron's Court.

Considering that David Lloyd is a man who rails against bureaucracy, detests interfering lawyers, and thinks the corporate world is over-staffed and over-stuffed with people employed to do needless and frequently obstructive tasks, it is amazing that he and Jarvis ever felt comfortable with one another. But Jarvis was at pains to insist that he understood his new partner a great deal better than a man in his position would normally allow.

'As I have said, I admire David and have a lot of sympathy for many of his views,' he says. 'There has, to some extent, been a coming together of minds and I do not find it difficult to agree with many of his beliefs.'

Whether that viewpoint was passed on in such emphatic fashion to Steve Philpott is open to considerable doubt. Philpott was selected as the lone Whitbread employee who would transfer to David Lloyd Leisure and assume Ian Taylor's position as Managing Director under Lloyd. As a keen all-round sportsman who has played football and cricket, rowed at Oriel during his Oxford days, and was now trying to do something about his golf handicap, Philpott seemed to have the right kind of personal credentials for the job, quite apart from the fact that he had made a big success of his role as Marketing Director overseeing the restaurant side of Whitbread's business. When I spoke to him in April, Philpott seemed well aware of the differences between the two environments and the need to treat a small company somewhat differently from a big corporation.

'I came from a very large company employing thousands of people,' he pointed out. 'There are, for instance, 300 Beefeater restaurants alone, yet here we are dealing with a concern that has fifteen units employing between sixty and seventy people each. It is a very young company and very naturally still revolves around the man who created it. Everything is much more focused on one individual and there is no right or wrong with that — it is simply the way the company has developed. It is important that David retain a high profile, but inevitably the Managing Director will have to play a larger role because David doesn't have enough hours in the day — even by his standards — to cover all the ground now.'

If Philpott had managed to convey that understanding to some of Lloyd's senior staff, some of the problems that followed might have been avoided. But the new MD was certainly right about one thing. Lloyd would have less and less time to visit all his clubs because, far faster than City analysts had predicted, there would soon be too many of them. As the expansion plans took wing through 1996, the City had based its assessments on a growth ratio of two or three new clubs opening every year.

'But by January next year we will have opened seven,' said Philpott. 'That will give us twenty-one properties going into 1997 and we will be looking for a 10 per cent growth rate in actual clubs over the next several years. Obviously we can't go on building forever, but we see a potential for about fifty leisure centres of this type in Britain. And then, of course, there is overseas . . .'

Newcastle, which was a takeover of an existing club from ITI, was up and running by the first week of May, and the others that were due to follow as brand new entities were: Sidcup in July, Stevenage in August, Brighton in September, Cheadle Royal near Stockport in December and Leeds and Milton Keynes by late January 1997.

As Peter Jarvis had pointed out, there was a marked difference in the way Whitbread had handled the acquisition of their two big purchases in 1995. David Lloyd Leisure had been left alone as a separate entity to an unusual degree, while Scott's Hospitality, the company that owned the British franchise to the American hotel chain Marriott, had been dissolved and their head office closed down within a month of the takeover.

'With Marriott we were buying a brand name we wanted to use for a specific purpose,' explained Philpott. 'With David Lloyd we wanted to learn from an expert in a specific field and then, with our financial resources, help it grow, so two totally different strategies were required.'

The reason Whitbread were so keen to get their hands on Marriott is interesting. Their Country Club hotels, while reasonably successful, were not attracting nearly as many American and Japanese golfing enthusiasts as they would have wished. The reason was quite simple. Country Club hotels had no brand name appeal. Few people had heard of it, and even those who had would never have mentioned it in the same breath as Four Seasons, Hyatt, Inter-Continental — or Marriott. Now the Forest of Arden and other hotels in the group will have that familiar Marriott logo in front of their names with all the connections to hotel, airline and rent-a-car award schemes that regular travellers and upmarket holiday-makers hold so dear.

The reverse strategy is being employed with DL Leisure because the name is already the brand leader in Britain. No need, nor any desire, to change that. And Lloyd would never have sold his enterprise had Whitbread not offered what he had considered to be cast iron guarantees that this would be the case. Within a matter of weeks Lloyd would be wondering why 'cast iron', when used to describe a guarantee, could turn out to be such a flimsy phrase.

Chapter 19

Buy Out and Blow Out

The deal nearly never happened. When David Lloyd arrived at Whitbread's head office in Chiswell Street one fine afternoon in 1995, he discovered that a clause was missing from the contract. It was the clause that was to have offered him a position on the main board of Whitbread. He had thought that was understood.

'I had made it quite clear to Peter Jarvis in our initial discussions that I was ambitious, and that I was not the sort of person who was going to grab the money and go sit on a beach. That isn't me. I felt I might have had some bigger role to play that would be of use to Whitbread, but when it came time to sign the contract, that part of the deal did not materialise. I don't know why. Maybe I misunderstood, but I usually make myself pretty clear and I felt let down. I've never been a great believer in contracts and most of my senior staff worked for me for years on a handshake. That's what I thought I had with Peter but, of course, I was now dealing with a corporation and the very board of directors I wanted to join. For some reason the collective decision had been not to honour that particular part of the deal and I suddenly felt differently about it. So I asked for time to think it over.'

Even before he had got through the door, Lloyd had decided to scrap the whole thing. There was always part of him that was tugging against the idea of selling his name and putting his company in someone else's hands, and he knew he would only agree to it if everything was as near perfect as he could hope for. That was no longer the case. In his eyes, a handshake had not been honoured and a position of influence had been denied him. Perfection was suddenly a long way off. So he started to walk back through the City to the Embankment, to the offices of J. P. Morgan, the merchant bankers, where one of his greatest friends, Terry Eccles, was Managing Director. Indignation was mixed with a feeling of relief.

Maybe it would all be for the good. He would be free again to run his own show, be master of his own destiny. The afternoon air put an extra bound in his step until, somewhere around Blackfriars, a nasty thought occurred.

'I remembered the shares. Although no one had cottoned on to the name of Whitbread, news started to leak out that we were ripe for a takeover and the shares had started to rise dramatically in the previous few days, going up from £2.30 to £3.60 which is a hefty increase. And I thought, "I can't do this, I can't walk away from a deal that will make our shareholders a fortune." My first priority as Chairman and Chief Executive of David Lloyd Leisure is to the shareholders and had I said, "No, the deal's off" because I didn't get something that was personal to me, I would be morally and legally in an untenable position. So when I got to Terry's office I asked him to phone Simon Burroughs at Barings, who were acting for Whitbread, and asked him to say that we were upset about something in the contract and that we would have to look at a different type of deal; a deal that would give us much more autonomy and have Peter Jarvis as the sole Whitbread person on my board with the promise of a main board position for myself at Whitbread within a year. After some further discussions we went ahead, both believing that we understood each other's position clearly.'

Although Lloyd does not want to characterise it in such harsh terms, it turned out to be as clear as mud. And it all centred on the appointment of Steve Philpott as Managing Director of DL Leisure. Lloyd is at pains to stress that what transpired was not Philpott's fault, in that he was doing the job that Whitbread wanted him to do. Despite paying lip service to David's extraordinary personality and the rare kind of company he had built, Philpott continued to do things in an essentially corporate way. The fact that he had never run a company before probably didn't help, but it was more the manner in which he did things that created the problems. He was a corporate man standing at the centre of an entrepreneurial wheel whose spokes were rotated by an amazing bunch of club managers who worked overtime for no extra pay as a matter of course —

managers who were used to taking decisions on their own and expecting a 100 per cent back-up from their Chairman even if they screwed up. Privately they might get the full brunt of Lloyd's wrath but publicly the front would be united.

If Philpott truly understood that way of working, he went about it in a strange way. It took him six months to visit Glasgow, where Donald Watt would have given him a very quick course in the business culture of a David Lloyd club. He did get down to Chigwell a couple of times but never took the opportunity to have a meaningful discussion with John Marnoch, another of the people who knew precisely what made David Lloyd, and therefore his company, tick. By the turn of the year, some four months after Whitbread had bought his company, Lloyd started hearing rumblings of discontent from amongst his senior staff. Decisions were taking too long. Decisions were being taken by Philpott at the Arena without proper consultation with the regional managers. Centralised management was creeping in; the long tentacles of the corporate machine were starting to strangle the spirit out of a dynamic group of people who were used to moving to the rat-a-tat beat of the David Lloyd drum. Suddenly they were having to listen to the Philpott bassoon.

'I should have trained him better,' admits Lloyd. 'The first mistake was probably on both our parts in that he was put in the job on a brief that neither he nor I properly understood. And then I just let him get on with it, which is how I tend to be once I've decided that the person is a good guy and has the talent. And Steve is a good guy, but I left him to his own devices too much and, naturally, he did things the way he had been taught. I tried to put it in tennis terms for some of my staff. I said you could liken Steve to Thomas Muster — terrific on clay but not nearly as good on grass because he had never had the practice and no one had taught him.'

For weeks, if not months, prior to the dramatic events that flared up in the middle of May, Lloyd had been listening to his staff and passing on his uneasiness to Jarvis. Perhaps Philpott wasn't in the right job, he suggested. Perhaps he might be moved back into the Whitbread corporate fold. The answer, to David's surprise, was a flat 'No'. At a meeting with Jarvis on Thursday 30 May he tried one more time. Then things started to get tense. The terrier was startling to bristle. The sleek bloodhound was heard to growl. These were two formidable opponents who, in over six months of direct contact, had never really tested each other's mettle. There had been skirmishes, differences of opinion and one near walk-out on Lloyd's part, but even then he had pulled back and Jarvis had never really seen him close up, with the fangs out, hind legs dug deep into his turf. Nor had Lloyd come face to face with a corporation who held so many of his personal aces before. Nothing is more personal than one's name and they owned that. He was no longer in full control of his destiny and it tore at his guts. Inevitably, the reaction was fiery and emotional. He stormed out of the meeting and called another, for his senior staff at Raynes Park the following evening. He was going to quit.

'I just couldn't sit there and watch the whole culture of our company change. If Steve Philpott stayed and no changes were made in the way he ran things, my staff would get more and more dispirited and I wouldn't be able to do anything about it. I was supposed to be Chief Executive Officer as well as Chairman, but suddenly I was being addressed only as Chairman in correspondence from the Board. It might seem like a minor thing, but it was huge when it came to contractual obligations and what sort of power I had to change things. It had all seemed so clear to start with, but there was something going on that I didn't understand. I didn't understand their intransigence and I thought it would be better for everybody if I got out.'

Senior staff from all over Britain drove or flew into London for what turned out to be an emotional evening. Well over a hundred of them were there when David announced that he would probably have to quit and tried to brighten the mood with quips about starting up again in six months under the name of John Lloyd. In fact, one of the many thoughts racing around in his head as he drove off to the West Country the next day to see his son Scott in Bristol and play golf in Wales, was to get Whitbread to fire him which would release him from the twenty-five-year ban on starting a competing business that was agreed when he sold his name. That would have been reduced to one year and, under those circumstances, he could indeed have started up under John's name with many of his senior staff joining him.

The idea had been talked about when David had taken some of his closest and longest serving managers off for a curry dinner after the meeting at Raynes Park. 'Yes, it did get a bit emotional,' admitted Donald Watt who had jumped on a plane from Glasgow when he got the call and had been disappointed that another senior member of his staff had not joined him. 'We talked about a lot of possibilities, of course, but the saddest thing was that people were starting to take sides. That had never happened before but now, of course, some staff members were afraid for their jobs and were trying to back the right horse. That didn't go down very well with me, I can tell you, and one consequence of all that was my decision to promote Gail Brown to joint assistant manager on my return to Glasgow. It was a reward for loyalty as well as for the fact that we couldn't run the club without her. And loyalty was what was needed at that particular moment. Otherwise some of us could see the David Lloyd Clubs being run in an impersonal manner and that would have been the end for a lot of us. If David had left, there would have been resignations, no question. And those who would have stayed would never have put in the hours they do now. It's David who gets us to work the crazy hours we do, no one else.'

This was a message that was starting to get through loud and clear to the Whitbread board. David Lloyd Leisure might be a maverick in their well-ordered stable but it was a productive maverick, a maverick, in fact, that performed like a thoroughbred when it came to nice, neat figures in the growth and profit columns. But if the jockey jumped off, then what? Would they be able to tame the beast and still keep it up to speed?

'Looking at it from Whitbread's point of view, you can see their dilemma,' says Terry Eccles, whose long-standing family friendship with David and Veronica does not cloud his thinking. 'They have this successful company that is highly dependent on one man who runs it in a way that is alien to them. So what happens if that man leaves? Obviously they were afraid that everything would fall apart if David left, and so they were busy trying to put an infrastructure in place that they could understand. It's the transition that is the difficult part, getting the balance right. Because, on the face of it, it does seem an extraordinary decision to try and change the way the business was run when it was so successful. It is just that the flat management concept doesn't fit very well with large corporations. David recognised that each facility within his own company was different and tried to make each club as self-sustaining as possible with just a few services supplied from the centre. That made a lot of sense.'

In the meantime, Lloyd was trying to make sense out of the whole sorry affair. A whiff of Welsh air helped and by the time he had turned the blue Ferrari back down the motorway towards Surrey, he had formulated a message to Jarvis that would put the ball back in the Whitbread court. 'I just left the door ajar a fraction,' he said. 'I really felt down when I left London and felt as if I was seeing the end of my dream, the dream of building something that I believed in and that had proved so successful. But then I thought that I owed it to a lot of people to see if a solution could be found.'

So, on the Monday, Sally Andrews, the personal assistant who sits in a small office just down the hallway from her boss at the Arena and somehow keeps track of his peripatetic lifestyle, drafted the letter that gave both sides a chance to take a step back and reassess. Later that week Lloyd found himself back in Paris for the second time during a sun-blessed French Open and still nothing was resolved. The first weekend he had been watching Henman and Rusedski try to come to terms with the red clay but now, over finals weekend, he was back as a guest of his long-time associates from Pellikaan in Holland. A lot of water had flowed down the Seine and through David's life in the intervening twelve days. But soon after he returned home, one more meeting with Jarvis and David Richardson, the Whitbread board member who had been a most understanding go-between during the difficult days, was sufficient to begin the healing process and ensure that the man with his name on the door would still be sitting behind the Chairman's desk. Eventually he was able to sit down and analyse what the fuss had been about.

'I think the whole problem was that at the beginning, the deal was done so fast. I think Peter Jarvis said the same thing: there wouldn't have been a deal done if we didn't respect and understand each other. Or at least think we did. Because I didn't really need to sell and I didn't really want to sell, but I felt Whitbread had a very good reputation as a well-run, well looked after, friendly company, which is what I wanted. And I think perhaps the mistake was at the beginning where maybe I didn't get to know Steve and he, perhaps, was put in on a brief that wasn't really understood by himself or by me. And what happened was we just sort of got on with our own ways which is how I tend to be. Once I know a person and think he's got ability and talent, I really let them get on with it and let them develop their style because it's their style that counts as long as it's around the same sort of culture. I think that's the difference between an entrepreneurial company and one that is very big. An entrepreneurial company grows from nothing and hopefully grows bigger and bigger. Therefore, everybody knows everything because they have to, and therefore it's a totally different structure from a big corporate body. And that is where the mistake was and I think, perhaps, I can see their point of view — if I did have to either disappear or not want to come back or get run over by a bus, the structure they understand would not have been in place. I believe the structure that is in place and the people I've got are actually fantastic and I don't think there would be a problem, I really don't, but that's obviously something that's coming from my side. I suppose if I put myself in their position, I could see that this is a structure they don't understand. Our structure changes daily according to our growth. You know, we don't put people in until they're needed and, at times, we are under-staffed, which is something that I know and the staff know, but we stretch and we really all put in extra hours, maybe eighty-hour weeks, if necessary, to cope with that mad rush.

'That's how we've always run the business and that's why I think it's been so successful because we've got the ability to put in those extra hours. And the staff actually want to do it. They don't get paid any extra. They don't get paid for overtime. It's the love of the company and the business that has allowed them to do that. And therefore, we've managed to get over all these major problems. I remember Dennis Brosnan, who was Chairman of the company when we had the four centres to do in one go, said, "Well, do you really have the manpower to do it?" and I said, "Well, I think we do." And we did. In fact, we opened three of them on the same day and we coped very well and everything was successful. It's amazing when people are put up against a wall — the type of people I have working for me — how they actually pull out the stops; how they work. The Donald Watts, the John Marnochs — I mean, these guys will do anything and that's what I think must be very difficult for a company the size of Whitbread or anyone else to actually understand. And I suppose I should ask, "Why should my culture be the correct culture?" Just because I think it is. I really do. I can see their point of view. But it's something I really must fight for because I think it's the reason that we have been so successful. And certainly 60–70 per cent of the staff, that have been there a long time, have this insane desire to work until the last pin is picked up. I mean, Donald, he can't leave the club if it's not spotless. It's something I don't think many companies have. And I don't want to lose that. And that's what I fought very hard for. And I think reading between the lines it was a total misunderstanding at the beginning. Perhaps I'm very different, but I just like to say, "Right. This is how we're going to do it. Put the cards on the table and do it." And that hasn't happened. Maybe they're frightened of me. I don't really know why, but at the end of the day, we've had a good fight. We've had a good punch-up and I think in all businesses and in all relationships, it's necessary to be able to do that — walk out the door and forget about it for twenty-four hours and then come back and either shake hands or walk. I do think that's something you've got to do.

'And I've said my things and they've said their things and I'm quite prepared to give it a go with a new structure in place. I think the staff have now got things that perhaps they were going to get, but they will get them quicker. I think the phantom share option scheme, which will be special to David Lloyd Leisure, will be brought in quicker. The bonus schemes will be looked at and the culture situation will definitely be looked at from both Steve's point of view and my point of view to make sure that it doesn't change. I think we've all learned a lesson and now it's important that we actually face each other and say what we really believe and shake hands and get on with it. I do that often and I'm quite prepared to do that. But I just feel everybody — the company, the staff,

Whitbread, myself — we had to know where the company was going and I think we know that now and I'm willing to give it 100 per cent of my time and effort to see that it does go forward.

'I said when we were taken over that my ambition was to make David Lloyd Leisure the most important sector within Whitbread. It hurts me when people say that they overpaid. It really bugs me because I know what the profitability prospects are. They didn't overpay. They paid the right price for us and they paid the right price for them to make a profit. At the end of the day in business, a deal can only be good if both people feel they've won. That's the only way. If there's only one winner, then the other guy gets pissed off and the whole thing falls down. I think we're both winners in this situation from a cash point of view, but I think perhaps no one quite understands how personal it is to me, that it is my name and it is my staff and I value them more than anything that money can buy. Perhaps people still didn't quite understand that and again, perhaps people didn't understand how much knowledge I have in the company. I know how the sewers work. If the jacuzzi breaks down, I can mend it. That's what I want all my people to be able to do. It's different but that's the way I want it and I believe that it's the right way. And so now we've got to look forward to see what happens in the next six to nine months and give it a full try.

'I think at the moment the company can't grow without me doing the day-to-day stuff as well. Perhaps I'm not the right guy to drive it forward and double its size. But I believe I am because I believe I'm good at what I do and I believe I can do many more things than just tennis centres. I suppose a problem from my side was that I thought I could be a bigger player in the Whitbread picture and that's been a disappointment to me. And maybe as time goes by they will find out that I can run any business; I mean a business is a business. I think my staff would do virtually anything for me. That's not because of tennis. That's because I think I get on with them. They know where they stand with me. I tell them "yes" or I tell them "no" and when I say "no", it's "no" and they don't argue. When it's "yes", they know I'm going to back them to the hilt. That I think is a very important management skill because a lot of people in management are frightened of saying things that might harm people and, therefore, they actually leave it with an innuendo which when misread is a disaster because you never know who's right and who's wrong. And everybody gets blamed for it. And I actually do think that sometimes you have to be very black and white. I'm a great believer in rotas just never being changed. Never. And I mean "never" and my managers would never ask me to change a rota because they know the answer would have been "No". And it's not being nasty, but I think it's the way to do it because once you let one person change it, I've got to let everybody change it. I can't say "yes" to you and "no" to another — I can't be like that. And therefore you have a disaster because you just can't pick and choose when you change a rota. I think a rota is sacrosanct. And these things are very important.

'It's the same with everyone pitching in and being able to do every job in the club. I honestly believe that in the year 2000 and onwards, you'll see more companies, big companies, being run like we run our small company. I really believe that. I do think it's the day of the track suit manager in all businesses. It's going to come because I don't think you can afford to have things any other way. You should be able to make decisions at the same time as running a business. I think I can make a decision while on the golf course or playing tennis. My brain doesn't stop. Why do we need all these meetings? The LTA is as guilty as most British businesses — they are always having meetings to decide things that could be agreed with a phone call. I do think it's going to change. And I think more and more businesses with the right people at the helm will be looking to get decisions made quicker at source and giving people at source more responsibility to run their businesses. I think that the area or the group roles have to be slimmed down. It's not just cost here. It's actually efficiency — immediate decisions. If you've got the right people, then you shouldn't change their decision. You should back them.

'Obviously there is a difference in running a service industry. But I think there are a lot of things that can be learned both ways and I'm sure I can learn a hell of a lot from Whitbread's structure as well. And I want to. Of course, I'm bigheaded. You know I think I'm the best. But I do learn and I want to learn. Even though when my father used to coach me, and said, "Oh, get out of it", and kicked me off the court, it did sink in and I used to go practise it behind his back so that he didn't know I was doing it. But I do listen, you know. And it's the hardest thing in life to admit you're wrong, especially for a person like me, but I do. I mean, sometimes you have to, but it's bloody hard. One of the hardest things I actually find to do is to say, "Gee, I've made a mistake here." But you have to do it. I think there's a lot to be learned from an entrepreneurial-type company and a well-groomed corporate structure. I think there's somewhere in the middle that both skills can be used to the benefit of the two. There has to be. I mean, we both have skills. And I'm very proud of mine and they're very proud of theirs. And that's why we had the row. We had two people thinking they were the best. When two people think they're the best, like a McEnroe and a Borg, they're going to have a fight. Let's pick the best of both. I mean, he's a professional. Peter and I have had long discussions and at times they have been very fierce, and when you're in arguments people always say things that perhaps they believe are true but perhaps aren't. Or else they're interpreted differently. But I think the beauty of people who really want to go forward is that you do learn and you shake hands and you go on. I've done that many times. The winner has to be David Lloyd Leisure which means Whitbread. And that's my staff, my name and Whitbread, and if that can happen, then we've all won. We've all got lessons to learn, and I think if we're all big enough to admit it, we've all made mistakes.

'There is no question things were taking too long and Steve and Peter and I have discussed this many times. The phantom share option scheme was something that took a long time. It was something that I promised my staff, you see. You can't have a share option scheme within David Lloyd Leisure because it had to be a part of a Whitbread share option scheme, and their policy is only for senior people which only my board qualified for and therefore the people down below didn't qualify. And I've always used the share option scheme as a bonus. Instead of a bonus, I used to give share options as a retrospective bonus which worked very, very well for everybody and they had a chunk of the company. So, I felt it was really important to carry this on and Peter Jarvis did, too. It was just taking too long.

'We both said there would be as much autonomy as you could possibly get and none of the divisions would be swallowed up by Whitbread. We both said it. They didn't really believe it. That's been the hardest thing for me to get over. Initially I said nothing. And I think they felt that if I left this would change. Well, that's something I had a long chat to Peter Jarvis about and he was absolutely adamant that if I went tomorrow, none of my divisions would be incorporated into Whitbread, which is the most important thing for my staff to know. Communication has been the problem because I've told them it would be like that and they didn't really believe me, and Peter's told them and they didn't really believe him either. We have to make a joint statement here. We haven't communicated. We just automatically assumed that he was doing this and I was doing that and that it all was hunky dory. Well, it hasn't been like that and the staff have felt it. Because Steve came in from Whitbread, it was automatically assumed that he was put in for a reason and what happened was you got sides. I've never had people taking sides in my life and that's what happened. And we've got to get the barrier down — no sides, no sitting on the fence. We're one team. And that's what I've been fighting really hard for. Basically, as far as I'm concerned, we're back to nine months ago. We've got a clean sheet of paper, which I'll give a 100 per cent go. The staff have got, I think, some backing from the fact that things will be done quickly so that they can be assured. A couple of people may get promoted onto the board which I think is very, very important for David Lloyd Leisure staff, and I think it's important for my people to know that they have a future somewhere — that they can go up the ladder and that they're not a number in a big organisation. And in my chats to Peter and by getting cross with one another, we found out really we wanted the same thing, but it wasn't happening at the same speed.

'I think it was a communication problem. We both went into corners and we each thought the other wasn't telling the truth. And that was tragic really and I'm very pleased it's come out and we both came round and knocked our heads together and said, "We've screwed up here. Let's get on with it." We both believe we had to bite a little humble pie here and there, and I'm happy to do that, and I think that's what's been sorted out. I really think David Lloyd Leisure has come out very much stronger than when it went in. And that's my job and that's what I'm paid to do. And in the end, that's beneficial to Whitbread, so they gain too. Everybody gains. At the end of the day, there may be a few people who might be bruised and battered, but I don't think there's any actual casualties. I don't carry grudges. I'll sit down with Keith Furphy, one of my senior people who started taking sides, and say, "This is what I think you did wrong. You might think I did this wrong, but I'll tell you why I did it." He might not believe me, but I think he will. We've all got a lot of things to do to make it right. You have to pull the people with you. You can't leave them behind and I think I'm good at that and, perhaps, I judge Whitbread as not being as good as me in that. Perhaps I should teach them. So, you know, I think we'll all be a stronger team, but at the end of the day, only time will tell.'

It had all come spilling out, the pain, the pride and the determination to make it right. He was clinging, as usual, to his creed; his way of doing things because it had worked for him and he was convinced it was the only way forward. He had established himself as an expert in his field and it was that expertise that Whitbread paid for. But with the package came the man himself, and if anyone ever thought he would steal quietly away in the night counting his cash they were woefully mistaken.

To be fair, Peter Jarvis never seems to have had any illusions on that score. When I spoke to him after some of the dust had settled, he was as understanding of David's position as he had been two months before.

'I know how strongly he feels that it is his name over the door,' said Jarvis. 'You spend your life building something up and you don't want to see it changed. But the fact is that nothing ever remains quite the same. No one can anticipate the difficulties until they experience them. But we have a decent relationship and have been pretty straightforward with each other. The business is doing fine and I am very, very pleased he is still there running it. I am certain the more we work together the more comfortable we will feel.'

Those were encouraging words but as Wimbledon got under way, it was still uncertain just how long David Lloyd would remain as Executive Director of his company. He was talking in months rather than years and the deal he had worked out with Whitbread over Australia was probably going to determine how long he maintained a day-to-day hold on proceedings at the Arena.

'John Alexander is going to be my Managing Director in Australia and I am putting in 25 per cent,' Lloyd explained. 'Whitbread also have a 25 per cent holding and we hope that the first club will open in Adelaide towards the end of 1997. It will require moving the old tennis stand at Memorial Drive, right next to the cricket ground, over to the other side of the existing Centre Court. It was condemned anyway and we will be leaving the forty-odd open-air courts as they are. In Sydney, the White City situation still has to be resolved but I hope we will be able to redevelop the site and bring a bit of life back to the place. It has such a fabulous history but I couldn't believe how down-at-heel it looked when I visited it for the first time last year.'

So David Lloyd, ironically for a reluctant flier, will be stretching his wings, finding new continents to conquer. It will always be that way. The house in Barbados will be visited from time to time as a holiday home, but the thought of Lloyd spending much time on the beach is ridiculous. No matter how many millions he accrues, the idea of easing up is simply not on the agenda. He has become a millionaire by really trying, not through the pursuit of riches but because of a burning desire to succeed. It is laughable how many non-achievers believe that money is the motivating goal, especially amongst professional sportsmen. Of course they want to make as much money as they can and their agents will see that they do, but a high percentage of them would still play tennis or golf or football whether there was big money in those sports or not. As Boris Becker, who could have retired years ago, was telling me before Wimbledon, 'I just love the game. I'm a fan. Even when I'm off the tour I watch it on television.'

This applies in the entrepreneurial world as well. To get another opinion on the David Lloyd phenomenon from someone who would understand, I spoke to Fred Smith, not a name that would immediately ring bells until you realise that his alias passes you everyday on the streets of most of the world's big cities. It is called FedEx. Frederick W. Smith had returned from the war in Vietnam to continue his education at Harvard with an idea in his head. He ran it past some of his professors in business school and basically received the same reply: 'Nice idea, young man, but you're out of your mind.'

So Smith went home to Memphis and set about proving everyone wrong. He set up his parcels business, based on the theory that the customer is the only person who matters, and Federal Express was born. His fleet of cargo jets and small vans now deliver anything, anywhere, anytime, on time. This is what Fred Smith told me:

'It has been my experience that successful entrepreneurship is almost always the product of near zealous devotion to a concept or idea. The success of the vision is the goal and the major source of satisfaction. Financial reward that accrues to entrepreneurs is generally the by-product of such concentration rather than the end in itself. Moreover, once success has been achieved, the nurturing of the enterprise and its continual evolution towards a higher state often continues to drive many business founders long after financial security has been obtained — sometimes many times over!'

Precisely. David Lloyd would agree with every word. Like Peter Burwash, the former Canadian No. 1, who has built up his worldwide network of highly motivated tennis coaches on the principle of service first, second and third, Lloyd is driven by the need to realise his dream on a recurring basis; to prove that his way works, technically, artistically and financially. In his book *A Wake Up Call for the Service Industry*, Burwash, working from first-hand experience, lists the companies that offer what he considers to be a proper standard of service. FedEx was one of them, the Four Seasons hotel chain another. None of the organisations he praises allows its employees to become bogged down in restrictive corporate practices. Everyone from delivery men to front desk clerks to head waiters is encouraged to make decisions and switch roles, if necessary, to help out a colleague.

This is the working culture that David Lloyd instinctively set about establishing in his company. Flat management, decentralised decision making, versatile staff who can turn their hand to any task, no clock watching and a real pride in your working environment — this is what David Lloyd has demanded and that is why his clubs have been successful. He firmly believes that big corporations, over-staffed with lawyers and desk-bound executives sitting in judgement on matters they know little about, will have to move towards his way of working. Challenge him on this and you will get an argument. In the early days it tended to be a lengthy argument based on conviction. Now the retort is short. 'Look,' he says. 'It works. I know. I did it.'

Index

Index

Index

Index